THE

CRYSTAL GAVEL

---

*How I Put My Heart into the
Body of the Law*

BY SUE COCHRANE

This is a work of nonfiction. It is a true story, told as faithfully as the author remembered it, to the best of her ability. Some names and details have been changed to protect the privacy and anonymity of various people.

ISBN 13: 978-1-63489-665-8
Library of Congress Catalog Number has been applied for.
Printed in the United States of America
First Printing: 2024
28 27 26 25 24   5 4 3 2 1

Cover design by Josh Durham (www.designbycommittee.com.au)
Interior design by Vivian Steckline
wiseink.com

To order, visit itascabooks.com or call 1-800-901-3480. Reseller discounts available.

THE CRYSTAL GAVEL

By Sue Cochrane

Contents

V.

PROLOGUE

THE DAY I WAS SWORN in to serve on the Hennepin County Family Court bench, I knew the rules—not just the ones for courtroom decorum, but also those governing personal and ethical behavior. The First Canon of the Judicial Code warns: "A judge should expect to be the subject of public scrutiny that might be viewed as burdensome if applied to other citizens." At that time, I had nothing to hide and was sure I would follow them all.

Five years later, after I finished my morning calendar, I found a package from an unknown address sitting in the middle of my desk in chambers.

I peeled back the brown mailing paper, opened the gift box inside, and discovered a full-sized gavel made entirely of hand-carved crystal. It was weighty and pleasing to hold. The handle was thick and cool. Sunlight refracted off the cut crystal edges of the round curves. Prisms of color reflected across the walls and ceiling of my chambers as I slowly turned the gavel over and over in my hands. It was breathtakingly beautiful.

There was a card with a handwritten message from a woman who had appeared before me a few years earlier. It was one of the more challenging family court cases I ever had.

The Third Canon of that Judicial Code I swore to uphold required me to immediately return any gift to avoid "undue influence" or even the mere "appearance of impropriety." I broke that rule. This is my confession and my long overdue thank-you card.

This woman's case had been eerily similar to my own parents' highly contested divorce. Like my mother, she suffered from chronic illness and could not work. She asked for decades of past child support and spousal maintenance that totaled over a hundred thousand dollars. According to her papers, the ex-husband had tricked the court for years into believing he was too poor to pay his support obligations. After many hearings by many different judges, the last one ruled that it was hopeless to try to collect from him. Yet here she came again, randomly assigned to me.

Like her ex-husband, my father never paid my mother any support after the divorce. He had a serious alcohol problem, but still was successful financially. The court did not help us either.

Mom was diagnosed with multiple sclerosis, and soon afterward, Dad moved out. She was forced to go on welfare with three young children when Dad failed to pay child support. Before the divorce they had three healthy children, a professionally decorated home, showstopper gardens that my mother created by hand, a lake cabin, two new cars, gourmet food, and an abundance of books, toys, music, and art supplies. After the divorce, we still lived in the house, but had no car, no telephone, not enough food, and for a long stretch, no hot water and no working toilet upstairs. We boiled kettles of water to pour into the tub when we wanted a bath. Mom suggested we pretend to be pioneers, which did not help. The house and yard fell so far into disrepair over the years, so full of weeds and dog feces that the neighbors called the St. Paul health inspector on us. I came up the walk to the house after school and a man jumped out of his official vehicle and handed me a citation and told me to immediately clean everything up. He said no one answered the door. I blurted that my dad was gone, my mom was crippled, and then started crying and ran into the house.

The woman in my court case gave up all her rights to the family business in exchange for generous support payments for herself and the three children. But right after their divorce was filed, the ex-husband quit paying the bills and everything went into foreclosure. His girlfriend bought his home and business at the foreclosure sale at far below market value and put it in a corporation under her own name. On paper he was a pauper. The previous judges all sided with him. In the last order the judge wrote, "The long history of this case shows that no amount of jail time will induce this man's compliance with the support orders. There is nothing further to be done. Case dismissed."

Now the ex-wife had something new. Someone had anonymously sent her a church bulletin announcing the marriage of her ex-husband and the girlfriend. She could finally collect what was due because everything became a joint marital asset. I reopened the case based on this new evidence and set it for trial.

"It's not true," the man testified under oath, appearing with a team of high-priced private attorneys. "We're not legally married."

He and his girlfriend had a "celebration of their love" in the Caribbean, with a private exchange of rings by the seashore. Upon their return, they lied and told the church and community they'd been married there. He testified that they resented being unable to marry due to the ex-wife's constant litigation, so they'd concocted this story.

After the trial and weeks of research, I made my ruling. Despite the precedent and the fact that they were not married, I felt driven to get those funds for the ex-wife. Although I had never seen this done before in family court, I officially added the girlfriend to the divorce case. I used the "rule of joinder," which was mainly used to streamline business litigation. Now the girlfriend was an equal party to this case and had to answer for everything she did with the transfers of money and assets. I also "pierced the corporate veil," which is just as it sounds, not allowing her to hide behind a corporation when wrongdoing is suspected. I learned this phrase in law school and loved it, but never thought I would use it. In my order, I made damning judgments like "sham transactions" and "fraud upon the court." But I did not feel as bold about this ruling as my written words proclaimed. My hand shook as I signed it. I hesitated to send it. Before mailing it, I showed it to several trusted colleagues. They unanimously said that the order seemed legally sound and well-reasoned, though unusual. I sent it out.

As soon as they read it, the man's attorneys wrote me scathing letters accusing me of abusing my discretion, improperly applying the law to the detriment of their clients, and of being an idiot (although they used legal words to say so). They filed immediate appeals to the appellate courts and hand-delivered a motion for a new trial to my chambers.

When I got those notices, I lost sleep, not because it was an unpopular decision—I made those every day. Something else about this case troubled me.

Sitting in the dark one night, I recalled how much I despised my father for not meeting his support obligations, which caused our mother to live in poverty without proper care for the rest of her life. For years after his death, judges would ask me if I was his daughter, and then they'd rave about him being the best trial lawyer they had ever seen. When my mother asked them for help, they protected my father. He constantly harassed my mother and broke into our home drunk in the middle of the night, threatening to hurt her. The police were called frequently but never arrested him. I remember one night after a break-in, a friend of his—who happened to be the mayor of St. Paul—drove over and gently led my father away to his long black car while the police officers waved goodbye.

Dad died prematurely when I was nineteen, and, thanks to his brother making the payments, left us three children a decent life insurance policy. When she heard this, Mom proclaimed he did more for us dead than he ever did when he was alive. She was bitter and angry at my father until her death.

I worried that I used this case and personal bias to seek retribution against my father on behalf of my poor mother. My colleagues did give me their objective assurances before I sent out the order, but none of them were in the trial, nor did they see my bench rulings or hear any of the testimony and evidence. I could have just followed the precedents set by the prior judges, and no one would have questioned it. The ex-wife probably did not expect anything different after all those other rulings. And, without a lawyer, it is doubtful she could have appealed the case.

There was one more similarity. In both cases, the mothers cut off all contact between the fathers and children after the divorce. This seemed beyond coincidence. I could not find peace of mind. I would just have to wait for the appeals court ruling to find out.

Before the appeal was decided, I had to take an unexpected medical leave to deal with a grave medical diagnosis—stage three breast cancer. My twin boys, Tom and Ben, had just started kindergarten, and our oldest son, Lee, was in first grade. The court administrator brought in someone to replace me temporarily so I could take the time I needed. I pushed the cases out of my mind, including this one.

My husband, Clair, a busy prosecutor, would take off work whenever I asked him to. But his job required him to be in court almost every day, and I knew how hard it was for him to arrange continuances on his trials because witnesses and police officers were lined up for weeks to testify. I liked tackling complex projects at work, so I did not mind planning and coordinating all the pieces of my breast cancer treatment and recovery.

The oncologist wanted me to start chemo before the winter holidays, but I pushed back. I did not want my sons' Christmas to be about my cancer, chemo, and nausea. She agreed it could wait until the new year.

I joined a chemotherapy trial because I wanted to receive Taxotere, a strong chemotherapy drug which then was being used only to treat stage four breast cancer. I figured the cancer was so far along that I could use that stage-four strength. The other drug was Adriamycin, often called "the red devil" due to its deep red color and its side effects: Besides nausea, diarrhea, and hair loss, Adriamycin can permanently damage your heart and burn your skin if even a droplet falls on it. The thick gloves worn by the nurses told the story.

After surgery and chemotherapy, spring arrived, and I began daily radiation to a large portion of my left chest and armpit. I have heard it said that women are "cut, poisoned, then burned" to rid themselves of breast cancer. The cumulative toll this took on me was frightening: Mouth sores made it impossible to eat at times; my favorite black tea with milk in the morning tasted like acid; I developed shingles all across my face, including the corner of one eye; I was bald and bloated; my chest burned redder than any sunburn. I dragged my body around the house and to appointments because the fatigue was overwhelming.

On my first day of chemotherapy, my oncologist set a bottle of one hundred Percocet tablets in front of me and said, "These will get you through." I was surprised. She knew I was a recovering alcoholic, with twenty years of sobriety. I questioned her about that and she said I would become "dependent, but not addicted." Over the next three months, I took every single one of those pills. Given the misery and pain I felt even while taking them, I do not regret it. When they ran out, I felt sad but it passed.

I was grateful to be home when the boys got off the school bus in front of our house at two o'clock every day. I took two Percocet before they got there, then reclined on our bean-bag chairs with the three boys sprawled all around and over me. We watched cartoons and movies on a giant television set my older brother, Dave, dropped off to help us survive. Clair would make hamburgers or microwave lasagna when he got home and joined us to eat and lounge together in the living room.

My final treatment concluded at the end of April 2002. The court administrator and chief judge called me more than once to see when I was returning. I told them about the post-treatment fatigue that was common in cases like mine and asked for more time. In the fall, I received a subtle ultimatum that if I did not return soon, they would need to replace me permanently. I went back.

I was still depleted, physically and emotionally. Having let down my professional guard for so long made it difficult to put it back up. Being a mom, not working, and focusing mainly on my healing was new and even pleasurable.

The day I returned to work, my hair was only a few inches long, coming in silver and wavy instead of light brown and stick-straight. I felt vulnerable and easily exhausted. My first week, one obnoxious attorney said in open court when I ruled against his client, "You must have chemo brain, your Honor." (I notified the court administrator that I would no longer hear cases brought by that attorney, an available option I never thought I would use.) Even a regular day without any upsets wore me out by noon. I would lock my chambers door, lie on the sofa, and close my eyes, but I could not sleep.

I heard that a part-time assignment had opened up to hear traffic court trials: speeding, red-light running, and driving without a license or insurance. No drunk drivers or hit-and-runs. A respite from the intensity of family court, where we worked in the middle of conflict, suffering, and violence every day. I asked the chief judge for the transfer and got it.

I packed everything up and left my expansive modern corner office, with its two walls of windows overlooking downtown Minneapolis, the Mississippi River, and the new library across the street where I loved to go whenever I had a break. I also had to leave my staff, friends, and colleagues behind. They held a go-ing-away event with food, photographs, and a gift certificate for a spa day. From there I moved into a drab office, about one-quarter the size of my previous space, where I knew no one. It was in the old courthouse a few blocks away. It had one small window. Although my passion and expertise were in complex family law matters, and my ego stung for a while in my run-down surround-ings, my intuition knew my life depended on this.

It was about a year into that traffic court assignment that the crystal gavel arrived. This is what the card read:

> Thank you for taking the time to read my whole file and re-open the case. After the appeals court affirmed your ruling, the lawyers settled the case with me and I got a lump sum. I can now travel to visit my grandchildren and get medical care. He got married. I have a life.
>
> I saw this gavel and immediately thought of you. I found out you were gone from family court and, hope you don't mind, but I made further inquiries. A clerk said you went through a serious bout with cancer and are back part-time doing traffic court. I pray for you and your family daily. Blessings.

How could I return her gift as the Judicial Code mandated, when she went to such effort? Especially since the legal case was truly over. This could not possibly be a bribe. I imagined how hurt she would feel to get it back. And I have to admit, I already loved it.

Yet the law said otherwise.

I gently put it back in its box and pushed it deep into a desk drawer to think about what to do. And maybe also to hide it. I never sent a thank-you card because that would have incriminated me. Sometimes I hate what the legal system has done to my thinking.

Months passed, and I felt guilty when I thought about the crystal gavel in my drawer. Mainly because I never wrote to thank her for her gift, but also because I knew I kept it in violation of the Judicial Code.

After a few more months passed, I knew I had chosen to keep it and decided I might as well enjoy it. I displayed it openly on a bookshelf. I looked at it every day, often picking it up and feeling its weight in my hand. I touched the cool handle and enjoyed the colors when I held it up in the sunlight.

Hardly anyone had occasion to visit me in my remote traffic court chambers, and when they did, they always admired my gavel. I never disclosed the source.

Occasionally the county sheriff's deputies would stroll over from the jail next door to chat with me under the guise of doing a "random security check." Looking back, I wish I had said I was busy that particular day, which I was, when one of the deputies came to visit. Instead, I smiled and let him in. When he noticed my bookshelf had sagged away from the wall from the weight of all the law books, he walloped it with his large backside to straighten it. My crystal gavel jumped off the shelf. It fell to the floor.

I knelt down to gather up the pieces with tears in my eyes. He sincerely apologized and I told him everything was fine, but that I needed some time alone and he quickly left. I picked up the pieces and held them. I was surprised the gavel had not completely shattered.

The crystal gavel broke into five separate pieces—the carved handle, the shapely head, and three round, identical jewel-like pieces. My heart hurt and my knees did too, but I stayed on the floor holding the pieces in both hands. Part of me thought the gavel broke because it was an illegal gift and that is what I deserved. My bad karma. Another part was angry at myself because I allowed this man into my chambers just to be polite and he threw his weight around and broke my beloved gavel.

The crystal gavel represented something deeply important to me, something that I could never put into words. I wondered what was so compelling that I broke the Judicial Code, so against my character, just to keep it. Maybe because this was nothing at all like the wooden gavel used by judges as an instrument of authority: One crack and a courtroom went silent. If you didn't obey it, you could be thrown in jail on the spot for contempt. I was never an authoritative judge, nor an eloquent one. I was just me, trying to do the right things. This gavel was clear, fragile, and beautiful. Feminine. Not meant to be pounded.

The law trained lawyers and judges to reduce people and cases to a legal problem. True or false. Guilty or not guilty. Important stories in the lives of the people who came to us for help were ignored. Feelings and emotions were considered irrelevant, including those of the judge. We were all supposed to leave our hearts at the courtroom door before entering.

I never tried to glue the crystal gavel together. It would not be the same. Even so, those pieces were still beautiful, although the edges were knife-sharp. I put them into the original box and into the desk drawer again.

Two years passed. I was called back to family court and felt ready to return. I unpacked and placed the box that held the gavel pieces on the shelf in my armoire, where I saw it every day when I put my robe on for court.

Five years later, I packed up my family court chambers once again, this time for the last time. The cancer had returned, metastasized to nearly every bone, and I received a terminal diagnosis. The oncologist said he did not know how long I had, but it would be cancer that would cause my death. He felt hopeful that I would see some milestones. I was not sure if he meant I would see all three sons graduate from high school, but I hoped so. I retired early, when I was fifty-six, in order to be present with my family for as long as possible.

About one year later the cancer went to my brain. I was diagnosed with an inoperable brain tumor. I took the gavel pieces out of the box for the first time since the day it broke. I placed them on a square of black velvet and moved them around like rocks in a Zen sand tray.

I leave the gavel pieces out on a table and change them every now and then. I let my hands move the pieces without thinking until a particular formation seems complete, for that day at least.

I

BULRUSHES

I FOUND OUT I WAS defective halfway through kindergarten. Walking home from school for winter break, I opened my first report card and read: "Does not speak or sing in class. Needs improvement in the second half of this year or will not pass into first grade." I pushed it back into the envelope, placed it on the kitchen table, and ran upstairs.

That night, my parents came to my bedroom together. They'd never done that before. My father, a trial lawyer, was still wearing his dark blue suit from court, starched white shirt, silk tie, and matching handkerchief in his chest pocket. I lay completely still, wishing I could sink deeper into the mattress and disappear.

They had talked this over, this business about me not singing or talking at school and said they'd buy me a really big present at the end of the school year if I would just sing and talk like the other kids. My father said I needed to show those old nuns how smart I was, and he laughed loudly about that. When asked if we had a deal, I nodded yes, and my father squeezed my foot and my mother kissed me on the forehead. When they closed my door, the scent of alcohol and cigarettes lingered. I pulled the blankets over my head.

I thought about how lucky I was to have my own bedroom, being the only girl. All my treasures were here: books, art supplies, xylophone, and a dozen stuffed animals. In a year or so every animal would have a name, a family tree, their own personality, and a distinctive voice when they talked. I wrote rhyming poems and gave them to my parents. My mother wrote the date on the back, saying that when I was older, I would really get a kick out of them.

After they left my room that night, I heard the familiar rattle of ice and muffled laughter. I hoped they did not have company over. I hated when they called us down to meet their friends.

"Here's my future law partner," Dad always said about my older brother, Dave. Then he went over and stood next to my younger brother, Mick, and said, "Here is our youngest, my namesake, Hamilton Edwards Cochrane, II, my junior partner." (Mick hated the name Hamilton and insisted that everyone, even Dad, call him by his nickname.) People smiled and clapped.

"And here is our Susie," Mom said, as she pushed me forward a few steps. I looked down at the carpet. "She's *shy*," Mom said in a stage whisper, as if I had some kind of dread disease.

When kindergarten resumed after winter break, my classmates stood to sing, as we did every morning. I stood with them, as usual, my lips grimly pressed together. As much as I loved music, and wanted to please them all, I could not even pretend to mouth the words.

Later that morning, Sister Mary read us the story of little Moses, turning the children's book to face us so we could see the pictures. Sister Mary read that Moses was found in a "basket made of weeds."

"Bulrushes!" I blurted out. The children all turned to look at me. "It says bulrushes, not weeds," I whispered, my head down, my face burning.

Sister Mary rushed out of the room, the giant wooden rosary attached to her side rattling. She returned with Sister Marie St. John to cover class for her. Sister Mary took me to an office, opened a thick book, tapped the eraser end of her pencil on a paragraph, and asked if I could read it. I could have, easily, but I pretended to stumble through it. When I finished, I looked up and was surprised to see Sister Mary smiling at me. I wished then that I hadn't held back.

I never sang with that class or spoke in that group again. Forty years later, frantically researching autism online after a social worker said our oldest son showed signs of it, I accidentally typed "mutism," and there I discovered the condition that had plagued me from that kindergarten class all the way through law school. Finally, I found the name and explanation for what I believed was my endless failure to fix myself.

When kindergarten ended, I opened the final report card on the way home, and saw that I got all plus signs, but one minus sign in the box next to "I can sing and talk with the class." When I got home, I took a ballpoint pen, drew a vertical line through the minus sign, and left the report card on the table.

After dinner, Mom left the room and returned wheeling a full-sized baby buggy, holding a giant baby doll dressed all in pink. She parked it in front of me.

"Congratulations, sweetheart," she said. "You did it! You are off to first grade. We are so proud of you."

This made me doubly sad because I never played with baby dolls, and because I lied. I didn't lie to get the present. I lied so they could stop being ashamed of me.

TWINKLES AND EFFIE

MY VOICE WAS TRAPPED INSIDE, and I was powerless to change that. I could not speak in school or public places no matter how much I wanted to. Calling me "shy" while making a face, my trial lawyer father and socially gifted mother seemed displeased with me. But, as I found out in my forties, this was not shyness: I suffered from selective mutism. Originally the condition was called elective mutism, implying the child willfully refused to speak. Many thought the child was faking, or being oppositional. It is well accepted now that children with mutism are truly incapable of speaking in certain circumstances, even though they can freely speak in others, and selective mutism is listed in the DSM as a social anxiety disorder. Without treatment or intervention, it rarely improves.

At home I was free to talk, play, and sing, depending on who was present. Dave had his own friends and interests, so Mick and I became close and played together constantly. I not only had my voice with him, I had dozens of others: I created a world of talking stuffed animals long before Sesame Street. Mick started it all with a wish for one giant teddy bear.

When he was about four years old, Mick wished upon a star. I was by his side, looking out his bedroom window at the star, and instead of keeping his wish completely secret like I advised him, he told me: a giant teddy bear.

A few weeks later, in early November, Mom sent me down the block to Mrs. Vornbrock's house after dinner. I did not want to go, but I could not even ask my own mother why I had to. I did not know this older woman, knew her only by sight, watched her visit Mom's rose garden or walk past our house on her way to the corner store. Obediently, I walked to her house and rang her doorbell. Without words and within minutes, Mrs. Vornbrock and I were on a bus to downtown St. Paul. We walked into a brightly lit drugstore.

"I am shopping for your mother to get Mickey a birthday gift because she doesn't feel well," she told me. "I suppose you are here to help." She pawed through a bin of cheap toys: tiny cars, rubber balls, and plastic magic tricks wired to colorful cardboard backings. My stomach tightened. I knew what he wanted and it was not in there.

I turned away from her. My gaze wandered around the drugstore, then up the wall. High on a shelf, near the ceiling, was a long row of giant teddy bears, maybe a dozen of them, each with a wide red bow around its neck. I saw the one for Mick right in the middle—he was a light golden brown, softer and fluffier than the others, or so I thought, glowing under the fluorescent light.

I looked over at Mrs. Vornbrock. She was still at the bin. My heart was thumping. I could not tell her about the bear, even though the words were crystal clear inside me: *There is Mick's present! That bear right there. He wished on a star for it and here it is! I found it! We must buy it for him right now.* I had no idea how much money Mom gave her, if any. I felt panic thinking that his wished-for gift was so close, yet would slip away. My being unable to speak was about to ruin my brother's life forever.

The next thing I remember is being back on the bus with Mrs. Vornbrock. Pitch black outside now, a cold Minnesota November evening, but inside the bus it was warm and bright. My arms were around the big bear. I squeezed his heart to mine, buried my face in his furry neck. My little brother's "Star light, star bright" wish had come true.

I do not know how I got the bear—did I point, cry, or whisper? Did I tell her with words? I may never know, but I am endlessly grateful I got him. One thing I do know—my love for my younger brother gave me the ability to communicate clearly at that moment, with or without words.

On his birthday, when Mick saw his big bear, he touched its head, and softly said, "His name is Twinkles, because he came from a star." The world of Animal Town was born.

The voices of the animals, their personalities, and their stories came easily to me. Speaking for them, I was never mute. Maybe this was a release of the thousands of pent-up words and stories I could not share before. I especially enjoyed singing for the animals when they were guests on the radio show.

More bears came along. Twinkles had a son, named Sunny. Another named Honey. The story I told was that they all came from the Milky Way, starting, of course, with Twinkles. They were called M-Ways for short. There was much more. They once were all real animals and were given a choice to go on "Inviso-Ray": They could leave the earth and zoom around the galaxy having adventures unseen. They knew they would someday have to come back as stuffed animals, but with a voice. They chose this adventurous path with passion and courage.

Also included in the M-Way family were any other cuddly mammals like rabbits, cats, and dogs. I had three identical, floppy white poodles with jingle bells in their ears: White Shadows I, II, and III. I had a black-and-white standing poodle called Daisy. A tiny one with real angora curls named Violet, after her color. She traveled in my pocket when we left the house. The poodles had soft voices like me and they were always happy. They were my favorites.

Over the years Animal Town grew. We had an anthem, a hospital (where I sewed up split seams and replaced eyes), a post office, a radio show ("Sing! Sing! Sing!"), a restaurant, and a presidential election (Twinkles always won). M-Ways were always kind and friendly. Fuzzy, one of the most energetic and popu-

lar Animal Town members, was the radio DJ with many singing guests. He also ran Fuzzy's Diner from the kitchen, which
annoyed Mom at times—she was trying to drink her coffee and
smoke a cigarette at the kitchen table in peace.

One Easter morning when Animal Town was flourishing, we
came down for our baskets of chocolate rabbits and eggs, and
there was a three-foot tall Mother Goose presiding over them.
She was not huggable—she had a plastic beak, plastic glasses,
a stiff skinny neck, and a scratchy bonnet and vest. She became
the first of the G-Way population (Goose-Way), which included
animals we received that were not cute, cuddly, or easy to love.

Goosey sounded remarkably like my father's mother, whom
we called Nana, a name she insisted we use. They both had an
affected English accent and a superior, cold attitude. No one liked
Goosey much in Animal Town, yet somehow she ruled the roost.

Until Effie, the magnificent red poodle, came along.

Effie's arrival was set in motion when Mom needed a dress for
some event, possibly a funeral that she had to attend. None of
her elegant tailored suits and dresses fit her anymore. She went
from slim to overweight in the year after Dad left. Every night she
stayed up making toast, drinking coffee, and smoking. Her symptoms from multiple sclerosis were getting worse. She suffered
from painful backaches; then the entire right side of her body
became numb. She occasionally had blurred vision. It was scary
to us because no one explained what was happening. Most days
she lay on the sofa with the drapes drawn. She quit cooking and
cleaning and gardening. We ate at drive-ins and lived on candy
and snacks. My favorite days were when she dropped us off at her
mother's, our Grandma's, house.

Dad began to break into our house at night drunk. Mom told
us that she thought Dad wanted to kill her. I think now that it was
the only way for him to express his grief and rage over all he saw
himself deprived of, including access to his children. We were
terrified and called the police when he showed up. She probably
sat up at night keeping watch for him. He would call over and

over and when she took the phone off the hook, he would appear at our house.

Mom moved less and less due to a combination of MS and depression. Her right leg seemed like dead weight. She manually dragged it forward every time she took a step. Her lush rose garden filled with weeds. The house became an embarrassing mess inside and out. Mom lived in a sweatshirt and sweatpants and had nothing to wear for any occasion. So I was surprised when, one summer day, she cleaned herself up and took me with her to Effie's Dress Shop.

Effie seemed to be about my Grandma's age. She wore a slim navy dress with a belted waist, her gray-streaked black hair in a bun. The dress shop was in her home, not far from ours. The living room had only a few chairs, but many racks of dresses just like a department store. The built-in oak bookcases and mantel held handbags and hats. Effie was kind to my mother, who was crying but still trying to joke, telling Effie she needed a tent or a muu-muu. Effie laughed. "Esther, you are funny!" she said. "And beautiful. Let's find you a dress that matches your beauty." She hummed and concentrated on selecting dresses off the racks, filling her arms.

While Mom tried them on in a curtained-off area of the dining room, I was transfixed by what was on a round oak table in the entryway. A gigantic red dog. A fishbowl, half-filled with small pieces of folded paper. A raffle for the most incredible stuffed poodle dog I ever saw.

This enormous neon-red poodle sat upright on the table, a square tail protruding from her cylindrical body. Black-and-white felt eyes the size of eggs and a stitched-on smile. The kind of grand prize you never win on the state fair midway.

I heard Effie say, "I will take this in here and here, and hem it, Esther dear, and you will look stunning. It will be ready one week from today." Mom looked happy for a change.

I tugged Mom's sleeve to show her this amazing creature. I pointed to the fishbowl. She filled out a raffle slip while telling

Effie about my shyness and how I talked through my stuffed animals. How I adored poodles most of all.

A week later, Mom came in the front door with a dress bag over one arm and the stuffed poodle under the other, like a red tree stump. "You won Effie's Dress Shop raffle, Susie! Here is the big red poodle." Mom held her out to me and I took her. She was heavier than I imagined. I hugged the giant red poodle as I lugged her up to my room. She was the biggest animal in Animal Town, and yet another poodle. Goosey shrank in comparison. It was possibly the best day of my life so far. I named her Effie. I imagine this might be what Mick felt when he got Twinkles the teddy bear.

Effie looked like a poodle crossed with a middle linebacker and she had the voice to match. She was a truth-sayer, and her guttural falsetto shout, which never varied, surprised even me as it came from my small frame.

No one in my family talked about what was going on. Dad was gone, we had no money, Mom was depressed, suffering from a frightening disease. Dave, now a preteen, showed the most anger at the dire circumstances: a drunken, violent father who paid no child support, a sick mother, no money for anything. Effie took a few beatings at his hands. But she was tough. Solidly built, tightly stuffed with sawdust, she was more like a battering ram than a stuffed animal.

Soon she sat at the head of the dining room table (Dad's chair, barely used) with a panoramic view of our home, family, and life. Unafraid of anything, she spoke (shouted) freely about all the "elephants" in the room that we never talked about: piles of unpaid bills and papers spilling over tables and shelves; the dishes from the cupboard unwashed and crusted over, stacked in cardboard boxes on the floor; mattresses in the dining room that we dragged down to be near Mom; and, for a time, no hot water. Effie made her pronouncements and Mom even laughed sometimes. I liked carrying her around the house in my thin arms, saying true things. "We need help around here! Call a doctor! Call a plumber! Call a lawyer!"

Effie brought forth a voice that was hidden, even from me. With Effie in my arms, I was big. I was bold. I was me.

PRETTY IN PINK

I WAS UPSTAIRS TRYING TO get my thin, sweaty hair to curve like the pageboy on the cover girl of *Teen* magazine. Opening the bathroom door to cool down made no difference. The thick August Minnesota air was not moving. I wore my one and only pink blouse because the lady next door told me once that I looked pretty in pink. I was eleven and about to see my dad for the first time in over a year. I missed him. Last time, my appearance didn't matter. This time, I ached to be beautiful.

"Sure," Mom snarled. "Go pretty yourself up for your father."

My hands flew up and the metal hairspray can clanked into the sink. She was in the stairwell, clenching two rails. All I could see was her face, in between the bars like someone yelling from a jail cell.

Mom hadn't been up those stairs in months. She'd gone from limping to using a cane and then a walker, seemingly overnight. She slept on the downstairs sofa.

Life seemed like a disaster, except for the fact that Dad was on his way. Mick watched out the window for him. Dave was still in bed. "I am not going anywhere with that prick," he yelled. Mom pleaded with him, saying she'd be held in contempt by the judge. This was her last chance to comply with the divorce decree granting him visitation. I was surprised to learn there had been other visits planned.

Dave got up. Mom was climbing the stairs. Dad was on his

way. These unimaginable movements gave me hope that things were finally about to change. Maybe Mom was getting better and could sleep upstairs again. Dad decided to be responsible and make a plan to visit us. Dave put his anger at Dad aside and chose to go along with us. Dad quit drinking, and maybe he was coming home. This was even worth getting yelled at. When we walked out the front door, I thought we looked like a real family, at least from the outside.

Dad's car reeked of alcohol. I knew he was supposed to be sober seventy-two hours before visits. I read it in the divorce decree Mom hung on the fridge with a magnetic strawberry. He took us to three different places: the airport, a country club, and a pitch-dark bar and grill called The Steak Pit. (Mom called it The Snake Pit afterward when she found out.) There weren't many places to drink on a Sunday in St. Paul in 1966, but Dad knew them well. Dave ordered plates of food and malts at each spot, leaving it all untouched. I felt sad watching Dad pay for it, but he never complained.

We made one last stop. The amusement park and zoo we loved when we were little. We walked onto the grounds, and right away Dad waved a man with a Polaroid camera over, put his arms around us, saying, "Smile, kiddos!" He handed the man some cash and put the photograph in his pants pocket. After a few minutes we left.

Mom was waiting at the door when we pulled up. I am sure she could hear the metal scrape as he drove the car up and over the curb. Dave ran to report that Dad took us to bars and was drunk. She refused any further visits with him.

As I got out of the car, he handed me the photo, which I still have.

"Here, Suzy Q," he said. "To remember your old Dad."

The next time I saw him, I was wearing a white high school graduation cap and gown as part of the Catholic school graduation ceremony. When it was over, my class filed out of the pews and walked down the center aisle of the St. Paul Cathedral in a stately procession. I saw Dad standing in the back, just to the left of the massive doors. I felt excited and proud that he came to see me graduate. He was wearing the tan cashmere coat from his years as a successful trial lawyer. It was frayed and dirty now. He looked like a skeleton underneath, and his skin was a sickly color. He hunched over a thick wooden cane. He was forty-nine years old.

Our formal line melted into chaos as they pulled the doors open. I saw blue sky and sun and wanted to rush outside with my classmates, shout and toss my cap, but instead, I slowed down and looked into my father's face. I desperately wanted something, anything, to show that he saw me after all these years, but his eyes looked through me. There was nothing there.

Pianos and Polkas

I. Pianos

ONE AUGUST MORNING MOM DROPPED me and Dave off at his first piano lesson, held in the convent across the lawn from the Catholic school we attended from kindergarten through eighth grade.

Dave was six years old and I was five. I remember being in the piano room with him for the entire lesson. The piano teacher, Sister Mary Joseph, was the music teacher for the school. Tall, thin, in full black-and-white habit, she was visible only from her eyes to her chin. She did not smile as I recall. First, she sat in the middle of the bench and asked Dave to sit to her left on the bench with her. She played middle C. The first note I ever heard on a piano was that middle C. In that small room with no rugs and bare walls, the sound of the note reverberated all around us. If I played that note today, it would sound exactly the same—middle C always sounds complete to me. It doesn't ask for another note to be played.

Next, Sister Mary opened a brand new book, creasing it to stay open on the music rack—a beginner's book with notes the size of nickels. She opened it to the first song and played it for him. It consisted of only one note—middle C. Each measure showed four identical solid black quarter-notes until the end of the song where the final note was held for four beats: a whole note (which paradoxically looks empty—just the outline of a circle). The song was called "Middle C March" and had a line drawing of a marching band leader leaning way back, a baton in the air, one knee up, and a feather in his hat.

I watched as the fingers on Sister Mary's hand curved and moved as one. Her right hand dropped down, striking middle C with her thumb. Holding the note, she lowered her wrist below the keyboard, then brought her hand up, and released the note as her hand lifted up. Just as that hand came up, the other went down. Over and over her long fingers and graceful ballet-like movement created an elegant performance with just that one note.

They switched places. Dave hunched over the keyboard and shook her off when she tried to straighten his posture. He pushed away her long delicate fingers when she touched his hand to arrange it in the classical position before he played. He hit middle C hard several times then crossed his arms with his head down and his bottom lip out. I watched all this from the corner of the room in an armchair, forgotten.

On the drive home, Dave yelled at Mom that he would never go back. They argued. He slammed out of the car. She sat still and made no move to leave. After a few minutes, I tapped her on the shoulder from the backseat. She jumped.

"I want to take piano lessons," I said.

Mom knew how much I loved music and bragged to people that "Susie can make music out of a broomstick." I loved my xylophones. I had two, which I set end-to-end. Two sticks with wooden balls on the end allowed me to play two-note chords. I loved making up songs. Mom bought me plastic toy guitars at the drugstore. I tuned those tiny guitars to a made-up chord that sounded good to me. The plastic tuning buttons popped out frequently with the plastic string still attached, usually after a few minutes of strumming. I remember starting over many times, jamming a button back in, retuning and playing until it popped out again.

After a few more moments of silence Mom turned around in the car seat, smiled at me, and said, "Yes."

I started the next week, taking my brother's place. Same teacher, same book, same one-note piece. A complication—we didn't have a piano. Mom said we would be getting one soon, but for now I would practice down the block at the Vornbrocks' house. That was uncomfortable for me due to my shyness, but I did it once or twice a week. I also laid a full-length paper keyboard Sister Mary gave me on our dining room table and practiced my form and my songs every day on that.

The book was moving too slowly for me. I longed to use both hands to play two notes together. Once I understood basic note-reading, I leafed through the book and realized there were no two-handed songs in the whole first book. We went through the book quickly and I got my second book. It was the first in a classical piano series. I cannot remember the name but I remember seeing the dusty blue cover with no embellishments—definitely a serious book. No pictures, regular-sized notes. As soon as I received the new book, I looked ahead. There it was, not too far in, a song called "Drifting," which used both hands at once. I loved the name.

Sister Mary gave lots of homework, rhythms to clap, scales to practice, songs to learn. I lobbied Mom for a piano. She kept saying, "Soon." Every birthday and Christmas from kindergarten through the primary grades, I hoped and prayed there would be a piano downstairs.

Usually we got one big present and a lot of smaller ones from Santa. One year I saw the big box, opened it, and saw a toy called Showboat. It was a large plastic boat made into a theater. It came with set backgrounds and cardboard characters standing in little plastic circles so that you could create plays on the Showboat. I understood why she got me that, knowing my Animal Town world. But these characters wore long dresses and carried parasols and the men had top hats. I already had my world of make-believe all worked out. I played with it, and I tried to love it, but I didn't.

The next year, my big present was a set of beautiful handmade German marionettes a foot tall. A boy and a girl with hand-painted faces and exotic clothing. I think the boy wore lederhosen and the girl had yellow pigtails and a smocked dress. I figured they were extremely expensive. I didn't know how to work them, and the countless fine strings got tangled so often I finally gave up on them. It made me sad seeing them all twisted up in the closet for years.

In third grade, near the end of the school year, my mom showed up unannounced after school and waved me into the car. "Susie," she said. "There's a surprise for you at home." Mom led me through the living room and into the dining room and there it was. A piano. A modern, gleaming, Jesse French walnut spinet.

Years later, Mom told me that one of my dad's clients, who had no money to pay his legal fees, refurbished this piano and gave it to my dad. I was surprised and pleased to hear Dad represented clients who couldn't pay.

The matching piano bench opened up with gold hinges and held my first two books. I pulled it up, sat down, and started to play random notes on the piano. It had a soft, beautiful sound.

From then on, the piano was mine. No one else in the family showed an interest in playing. As I got better, I sometimes opened the dining room windows and played "America the Beautiful" as loudly and dramatically as I could, imagining some ladies from the PTA walking down our alley might hear and invite me to play for a meeting. I picked up the new songs in my lessons quickly, could play by ear too, and dreamed of being a famous pianist.

I never became a classical pianist. I didn't major in piano in college. I didn't even make it to eighth grade with my lessons. By the time I was in fourth grade, we were spending many weekends at motels hiding from my father. It seemed like every week or so, he came over late at night, drunk, and we were all afraid of him killing Mom and hurting us. Maybe he wanted revenge, maybe he wanted reconciliation, maybe he was just desperately lonely. One of these times, Mom heard clattering in our garage and then right outside the back door. She woke us up, told us to be very quiet, and without any lights on, stuffed clothes in a bag and whispered to meet her by the front door. Just as we got downstairs, we heard glass breaking at the back door and saw Mom trying to keep Dad's hand from reaching through the broken window to turn the lock. She said, "Run to the car!" We all jumped in and she raced us out of there. When we checked in at the motel, a Howard Johnson's or Holiday Inn, we saw Mom's hands were bleeding. She told us that Dad had taken the axe from our garage and used it to break the back door windows. I was terrified of Dad after that, and for years afterward, I had nightmares about violent break-ins.

The rest of the weekend we distracted ourselves with swimming and doing cannonballs into the pool. I loved how we ate all our meals in the coffee shop and could order whatever we wanted. I can't imagine how Mom paid for those motel weekends. On Monday, reality returned. Piano lesson day. I hadn't practiced all weekend.

I was supposed to be working on a classical piece to play at the fourth grade recital and felt special to have moved beyond the childish songs. Even the name was complex—"Berceuse." A few weeks later Sister Mary said I couldn't play it in the recital because I had not practiced enough. I had to play "Indian Pony" instead, from the second grade recital. I was crushed when she told me, but kept my face frozen. I raced home and told Mom, ashamed and in tears. I suspected Mom called Sister Mary and negotiated a deal that I would practice diligently from now on, because suddenly I was allowed to play "Berceuse" in the recital. Sister Mary and I never talked about it. I am sure Mom didn't tell her what was happening at home. Everything was a secret and we all knew to keep it that way.

I played "Berceuse" in the recital. I made mistakes right away and got flustered, but I kept going and finished it. I rushed off the stage without a bow. After that, I switched to a piano teacher near Grandma's house, a retired woman who mixed discipline with flexibility in a way that worked for me. I continued piano lessons for about five more years, but I never developed the discipline to practice and learn the harder pieces. I had a good ear but that made me frustrated when I could not play the songs immediately without mistakes. I started playing guitar and banjo—folk songs and fancy fingering—thanks to lessons on public television after school and my music reading abilities. I was too shy to sing, so I decided I had to become proficient on the instruments. I mailed in for the guitar tablature and found a new passion.

Around this same time, Aunt Marie, Mom's older sister, gave me all her popular piano sheet music from the 1940s, over a hundred pieces of them. I loved spreading them out on the floor, looking at the artful covers, choosing one to play that day. I learned songs I had never heard before—"Beautiful Dreamer," "Old Man River," "Bumble Boogie"—and I was happy with my playing again because the music was not difficult and I could hear the melodies right away without much practice. By seventh grade I was ready to ask Mom if I could quit piano lessons. She said, "Sure," and that was that.

At first I was relieved, but later in life, I regretted quitting. I would have liked to learn a classical piece, but I didn't have the patience to do it on my own.

I did learn Appalachian frailing style for banjo, and many styles of guitar: blues, electric bass, beginning jazz guitar, folk, fingerpicking, and I took classical guitar lessons in my thirties. I could listen to records and pick up most guitar songs by ear, like "Classical Gas" by Mason Williams, popular when I was in high school. I enjoyed playing banjo, guitar, and bass, but felt sad for squandering a talent for playing piano.

I didn't force my children either when they wanted to stop their music lessons. I suppose if we are destined to be concert musicians, we will be called so strongly that nothing will stop us. Now I am grateful that when I am alone, I can sit at my sons' modern electric piano, improvising chords and rhythms that seem vibrant and pleasing to me.

II. POLKAS

I was studying in a corner of the college student center when Al approached me and sat down. He was a tall, fresh-faced young man with black glasses. He looked a bit like Clark Kent. While I wore torn faded jeans and flannel shirts, he wore khakis and button-down shirts tucked in with a narrow leather belt. We were casual friends in political science classes and were in a study group together. He was majoring in public administration. We never socialized outside school, but I knew he was kind and had a dry sense of humor. He said he had an opportunity for me. "I started a band to play at weddings," he said. "I heard you are really good at the twelve-string guitar. Would you like to play bass guitar in my polka band?"

This was Minnesota in 1975. Polka band weddings were big. I had been to many, and being half German, I knew the words to a few polka songs and also how to dance the polka. With German maternal grandparents, I even knew all about Whoopee John Wilfahrt and his famous family polka band from Minnesota. But never did I once think about playing polkas in a band.

"Sorry, Al," I said. "I can't, I have never played bass."

"You play twelve-string guitar," he said. "The bass only has four strings. How hard can that be?"

He made me laugh as he often did, and I said I would think about it. I went downtown that afternoon to look at a bass guitar at Schmitt Music.

In the store, I tried several and played the blues runs I knew from the bass notes of my guitar. I was very self-conscious to hear my notes coming out of an amplifier, but no one was paying attention. My fingers needed to practice stretching to reach the notes on the long neck, but it was familiar enough. I decided on one by its looks alone: a sleek white Fender Jazz bass with black trim. I grabbed a beginner bass book on my way to the counter.

I asked if they had any polka books. For tuba. (It never occurred to me to ask for polka books for electric bass. I just assumed they didn't exist.)

"Yeah," the clerk said. "All the band music is upstairs." I asked him to hold the white Fender for me. I was noticing that I was feeling the same joy I felt when we got our piano.

There it was. A small five-by-eight-inch book, Whoopee John Wilfahrt's polka and waltz music—for the tuba. I could still read music, and I could easily convert these songs to the bass. Bass was easy, I thought, because you play only one note at a time. My first one-handed piano pieces were coming in handy now.

I bought trumpet and saxophone books for the other band members. Next, I looked at bass strings. Downstairs I had seen some black nylon strings I thought would give a soft jazz sound and blend well in a band. Truthfully, I thought they would look cool against the white guitar. I could be a punk rocker in a polka band.

At our first practice, with Al in charge, we sounded great. We were now the Al Anderson Combo. He played trumpet, and we had a drummer, a saxophone player, and a keyboard player. Even a female vocalist occasionally. Only the sax player went to our college, a year ahead of me and Al. The others were from Al's church.

Al was impressed and grateful I got the Whoopee John books for us all. I had even figured out the music for the piano player— just three chords. I found out I loved playing bass. Always shying away from solos or microphones, I now had a strong and important presence, but I was still in the background. My rhythm, fingering, and ear for tuning was noticed. Within minutes, in the Hamline band room, we whizzed through the polkas and waltzes. We moved into Neil Diamond's "Sweet Caroline" for a slow dance and "Proud Mary" for our fast dance rocker, the one where the bride dances wildly adorable steps holding her bridal train in one hand and a glass of champagne in the other.

That was a wonderful year. I played in a band onstage for money. I was in the back and off to the side, joyfully moving my hand up and down the sleek neck of the white bass with black strings. (Once when I was feeling low and wondered if I made any difference at all in the band, I stopped playing in the middle of "Satin Doll." One by one, the band members began to hesitate, fumble, and look around, and soon everyone quit playing, some swearing under their breath. I was in the back, laughing now, and they all figured it out. I never questioned my role again.)

Al was tall, muscular, and charismatic. He got us all our bookings. Gabe, the sax player, became my first boyfriend. Gabe was just as tall, leaner, and played like a pro, and he was gifted at improvisational riffs. He also had an excellent singing voice and could harmonize with anyone.

After months of him haranguing me, I allowed Dave to play guitar with us. He had been in a garage band, and I later regretted allowing him in. I had taught him a little bit of guitar when he was nineteen. Now he wanted to be the lead electric guitar in the Al Anderson Combo. The sounds he made hurt my ears, but I never could tell him. Before Dave joined us, we were an ensemble, and we coordinated our efforts to get the best sound from our group. Dave had a different agenda. He wanted to be a rock star. One time, after he played a loud lead guitar on a Rolling Stones song (done to a polka beat), the bride's father threatened to not pay us if we did not get back to regular polkas and waltzes. Our combo fell apart, and I felt responsible.

Gabe and I migrated over to Dave's garage blues band. We never made money again. We sent our tapes to a few professionals but never got a response. Everyone in the group had a college degree and we felt doomed to go on to graduate school as a second choice—at least I did. I knew I was too shy to stand up in front of a high school class as a French teacher, but French was my love, after music. My French professor, Dr. Root, assured me

I could get into the doctoral program at Stanford. I was not sure about that choice either, because I sometimes felt a stirring to help people who had been disadvantaged like me and my family. Reading ancient texts in French and analyzing them did not seem like something I would be happy doing for the rest of my life. When I told Mom about possibly applying to Stanford graduate school in French, she reminded me that I had promised to go to law school and asked who would take care of her. It was then I knew I would probably end up in night law school like my father, living at home and taking care of her. At least I would have a career and not end up on welfare like Mom did. Maybe law school would force me to get over my shyness too. I thought maybe I could be a lawyer who helped people like my mom. I still had Dad on a pedestal with his reputation as one of the best trial lawyers, wearing his expensive suits. But it was a male-dominated profession, and when I thought about Dad's reputation as a lawyer, it was hard to imagine myself as one. I decided to take the LSAT anyway—and a year off from school after graduating from college in the hopes that the right answer would appear.

The garage band played a few more yard parties but mainly hung out in someone's basement to play, mostly improvisational blues and rock. Someone would bring alcohol and I would drink until I was drunk by the end of each session. The band drank or got high, but I do not remember Gabe doing that. Despite my getting drunk every time we gathered, Gabe was wonderful to me. I met his family, learned how to downhill ski, and loved being near him. When he went off to graduate school in another state, he sent me witty letters, a poster-sized drawing he'd made of me playing the bass, and even some original poems. I had not heard of *The Lord of the Rings*, which shocked him. He gave me a golden box set, and I loved it as much as he did. When he came back for his first visit at winter break, I was halfway through my year off after college.

We went out to eat and I got drunk as I did whenever I drank. When he pulled up to my house to drop me off, he took my hands in both of his. He gently told me that he had met someone in grad school, and it was going to be permanent. I hung my head. Pangs of regret shot through me for drinking so much and losing him. I could not say a word or make a move to get out of the car. As he held my hands, he tenderly moved his long, artistic fingers over mine.

"Like rereading a favorite book," he said. He had tears in his eyes.

I still could not say a word. I got out of the car and walked up to my house. I watched from the living room window and saw that he stayed there for ten minutes before driving away. Even after his taillights disappeared around the corner, I continued staring into the night. The dark years were just beginning.

II

THE THINGS MY FATHER GAVE ME

A WEEK AFTER MY HIGH school graduation, a man came up the walk to our front door. The doorbell rang. I was afraid it was my dad. A deeply ingrained response, after years of him trying to break into our house after the divorce. But I remembered how weak and sick he looked in the cathedral at my graduation and, as the doorbell rang for the second time, I decided not to be frightened of him.

I cracked open the door. It was not my dad, but a short, thin man about his age. He spoke through the screen. "I have something for you from your dad," he said. I opened the screen door, and he handed me a keychain with two thick silver car keys on them.

"He is over at the Cherokee Tavern and asked me to give this to you," the man said. "He told me to say, 'Congratulations, Susan, this is your graduation gift.' Look." He pointed to the curb. There was a midnight blue 1967 Mustang Fastback. "I'll walk back," he said. "It's just a couple blocks. Have fun."

Staring at the car, I was stunned and joyous. "Please tell him thank you."

"Sure, I will." He turned and walked away. I yelled to whoever was home, "Dad gave me a sports car! Come here! Hurry!"

I rushed outside and walked around it. Ran my hand over

the warm, sleek body, shining in the sun. It looked to be in mint condition, even though it was six years old. I swear the paint had sparkles in it. The wheels were customized, gleaming silver. I opened the heavy steel door and sat behind the wheel. Sky-blue leather bucket seats. Immaculate. I touched the dashboard, clean and cool. I inserted the key and turned over the engine. It sounded to me like a semi-truck engine rumbling under the hood. It was powerful—a high performance, V-8, 289-cubic-inch engine.

Mick came running out. We had been without a car most of the time after Dad left. We sat in the leather bucket seats, turned on the radio, tried all the buttons, and honked the horn.

Mom was at the door, gripping her walker, waiting for us. As soon as we got inside, she started to yell. "You are giving that back right now. That miserable sot thinks he can put us on welfare for ten years, then give you a goddamn sports car and all is forgiven?"

"But Mom," I said. "You know I need a car to get to work. You say all the time it isn't safe for me to walk home at night after dark." I got a job as a waitress in a drugstore diner when I was sixteen, through the welfare department. A horrible job for a shy person at first, but it actually helped me break through my anxiety of talking.

I took a deep breath. "You begged me to stay here and commute to college instead of going out of state. Well, a car will help me do that. It will help us all."

"No!" She reached over her walker with her slow, numb right hand, trying to grab the car keys from me.

I resented seeing my mother choose to hate my father rather than letting me feel special with his spectacular gift. The fact that Dad tried again, after what Dave had done to him after his own high school graduation, was a miracle. Dad told him he had a great car for his graduation gift. They planned to meet at a certain intersection in downtown St. Paul. Dave went, but came home on the bus. He told us, grinning, that Dad showed him the car, a large fairly new sedan, then handed him the keys. Dave said that he walked over to a sewer grate, held the keys above it, and smiled right at Dad while he dropped them in. He headed for the bus stop without a word.

And there was one time after that, when Dad—who looked way too thin and was using a cane—rang our doorbell. Dave, a two-hundred-plus-pound defensive tackle in high school, opened the door, and, with no warning, shoved Dad, knocking him down onto the concrete steps. Dad's arm shattered. Dave joined Mom in her absolute hatred of Dad. They thought he was evil.

Somehow, Mick and I still felt love for Dad. We wanted him to get sober and to come home. I wanted Dad to love me. I wanted him to see me as special, smart, and talented. To me, the Mustang seemed to say that maybe he did. I used to think Dad was so important, going to work with a briefcase in each hand and a Camel cigarette dangling from his lips. Mom pinned a fresh rosebud from her garden to his lapel when he had jury trials. It was his signature look. I often asked Mom, "If he stops drinking, will you take him back?" She wouldn't answer me. After about five years of that, she said, "His brain is damaged now. Even if he sobered up, it would not improve. He's not the man I married." I was surprised to learn about the permanent brain damage. Her telling me this hurt me, but it also was good, because I could stop fantasizing about a happy ending.

When I was very young and Dad still lived at home, I sensed that he thought only boys and men were worthwhile and girls and women were just here to cook, clean, and look sexy. He'd comment on my appearance, especially my legs, which he often complimented. His attention made me self-conscious and want to hide from him. I refused to wear the skimpy sun suits Mom bought that tied in bows at the top of the thigh. He bragged that my brothers would be law partners. I never heard him say I would be one, too. They would go to Harvard. There was no mention of my future. I even put in my high school yearbook under my photograph, "Plans to go to law school." I had no idea if I could, but I did not want to be excluded and hoped somehow he could understand that.

When I was a bit older, I wanted to dress like my brothers. (I ended up doing just that.) I only wore braided pigtails and never wore my hair curled or in a ponytail, or straight down my back like Mom begged a few times. Just braids. I wanted to believe Dad loved me for who I was.

In Catholic grade school, I was surprised to learn that sinners could be forgiven in an instant just by asking. Even on their deathbeds, like the two criminals on the crosses next to Jesus. I pictured Dad, the atheist, this person who hurt so many, asking for forgiveness right before he died, and then being allowed to go straight to heaven. How unfair, I thought, when we had to follow the Ten Commandments every day to get there. This must be how Mom saw me—forgiving Dad the moment the car arrived. Maybe she was right. How dare I wipe out his abandonment, violence, and destruction in one moment because of his single grand gesture? I was pulled apart. I remembered a story that Dad was supposed to buy Mom a "nosebleed red" convertible in the early sixties, but the drinking and abuse were escalating and it never happened. I wondered if he got me a Mustang to hurt Mom and make her jealous.

Although both Mom and Dad came from poor Depression-era families, by the time they married in their late twenties, they both dressed in stylish, tailored clothes. I know they admired Jacqueline and John Kennedy, and I think Mom imitated her style. She was extraordinarily thin in photos from the forties, when she posed in a bathing suit and in professional attire with pencil skirt, heels, hat, and gloves. She wore deep red lipstick, drew her brows into dark arches, and wore her hair in a bun, which made her look older and elegant. Dad was handsome in early photographs, with black hair, a soft face, and loose, rumpled suits. Later he would wear sleek casual clothes from the sixties that Mom gave him—zippered pullovers, colorful cardigans (some with suede inserts), Ban-Lon golf shirts, and even a jumpsuit that looked like he could parachute in.

When I was young and looked through the boxes of black-

and-white photographs, I thought they looked like movie stars. It was not surprising Mom wanted a red Mustang convertible. By their mid-forties, however, both my parents would be completely unrecognizable from the modern, well-groomed couple they once were.

Keys in hand, I turned away from her and walked out the door. I had never opposed her before, not like this. I heard her yelling behind me to stop. I drove to the drugstore diner where I worked and showed my Mustang to everyone who was on duty. Waitresses, the cook, store cashiers, and even the store manager ran out to admire my new car. Some of my regular customers even came up to congratulate me before heading into the store.

I'd worked there two years—they all knew most of my story. I was hired the week I turned sixteen on a welfare-to-work program. I had no choice. Someone had to make some money for the family. This was a popular local drugstore fountain and grill, and it turned out to be the only job I had before my legal career. I started to learn how to talk to customers, co-workers, and managers. I had money—$1.60 an hour, union wages for the Hotel and Restaurant Workers Local in 1971. I got a major discount on drugstore items and provided things our family needed, like toothpaste, shampoo, and aspirin. I bought a small stereo for my bedroom, make-up, pantyhose, drinks, and snacks. I felt expansive for the first time, thanks to the job. Mick came there to visit me often, sat at the counter, and ordered his favorite item, the Supreme burger (a cheeseburger with criss-crossed bacon in the melted cheese). I made it with extra fries, no coleslaw, and never charged him. I even had a few dates with Len, one of the stock boys, a year older than me, who went to a public high school. I asked him to my senior prom, and it went fine. He was extremely outgoing, wanted to be a radio DJ, and was not self-conscious like me. My co-worker Carol's mother sewed me a long dress in the fabric and pattern I chose. In many ways, that drugstore diner was my home.

It was not easy starting that job; in fact, it was terrifying. I was coming out of a dirty, broken-down house that no one besides my family could enter, and I was full of secrets. I was struggling with my weight, possibly because we mostly ate fast food and ice cream and I drank endless sodas. I started many fad diets, sometimes starving and throwing up, trying to get thin, and often made it there for just a few months. I could not maintain the low weight, and started smoking cigarettes, thinking that would help. Only when I went to France in college, ate fresh food, and walked miles every day (while smoking) did I find my way to a healthier weight. Then as my drinking increased, I lost weight without trying, because I cared more about drinking than eating.

Carol, who trained me there, was a year older than me and a devout Lutheran who did not smoke or drink. On the first night, when I was scheduled to close down the grill, fryers, and fountain alone, she left me a handwritten three-page letter taped to the top of the grill fan to guide me though every move because she knew I was scared. Every year for thirty years after we parted ways, she sent me a Christmas card with a photo of her family. When I was drinking way too much in college, she gave me a holy card of Jesus, his hands held out, his eyes soft and loving. The quote under the photo said, "Ask and Ye Shall Receive." Six years later, when I hit bottom, that card may have saved me.

My work friends were as excited as I was that my dad finally came through with something good. They said Mom would get over it and I had to keep it. I recalled she got over two other gifts Dad gave me when I was younger. In eighth grade there was a round, sterling-silver pendant watch for my birthday, delivered by taxi, which I wore around my neck every day for years. I was the only one in school who had one. It stopped working sometime in college and I never got it repaired and lost track of it. When I was a lawyer, I bought a similar one and wore it every day. Later, I made sure to wear it in our one-and-only family portrait with our three boys when they were preschoolers.

When I turned sixteen, a delivery driver brought me a tiny jewelry box, wrapped in silver paper from a fine jewelry store in downtown St. Paul. Inside was a pearl ring, surrounded by a delicate, sterling-silver flower, perfect for a teenaged girl. I wore that ring proudly to my Catholic high school, a feminine contrast to the blue blazer, heavy wool-plaid pleated skirt, and navy oxford shoes. It caused a bit of a stir. Some thought I had a boyfriend. (Not even close.) I still have the ring in a box with my dad's wedding band, which he left on the kitchen counter when he moved out. My mother began to wear his wedding ring instead of her own after her hands swelled up from MS. I think she still loved him and hoped he would come back. A nun handed the ring to me at the hospital when she died in my first year of law school. I quickly put it on so I would not lose it, and I wore it on my right hand for years.

I also ended up with a soft, leather-covered book with onion skin pages, not much larger than my hand, that had been in our living room bookcase for decades. I found it in a box when I was in my thirties while moving from one apartment to another. Dad's name was written inside the front cover in his distinctive Palmer Method style with ornate first letters, and there was a single red ribbon marking a chapter. Once I opened it, I could not stop reading. The book was *Meditations* by Marcus Aurelius. I was surprised Dad had such an inspirational book and wanted to believe it was because he aspired to live a better life. The leather cover is crumbling now, but the onion skin pages are perfect. I have several paperback versions on my bookshelf and am still moved by the words and the author's life story.

It was an ugly few weeks after the Mustang arrived, but I held on to those keys. I drove off with my mom mad, I came home, and she was still mad. The angry silence pervaded the house. I stayed in my room when I was home, and I kept leaving whenever I could, sometimes just to drive around alone. I had friends, freedom, and admiration now. The guys at the gas station offered me a thousand dollars cash on the spot for that car. I smiled every time and shook my head. Two of my waitress friends had boyfriends who owned muscle cars, and they showed me how to change the spark plugs and oil. My friends and I washed and waxed our cars every week at the modern car wash, where guys flirted with us and envied our rides. This was my car, not a boyfriend's, which seemed to impress people. My waitress friend and drinking buddy Darlene and I drove "the loop" on Saturday nights in downtown St. Paul: she in her boyfriend's blue Chevy Nova with jacked-up mag wheels and me in my Mustang Fastback. We gunned our engines in neutral at red lights, looking over at the guys in their Chargers and Camaros next to us. When the light changed, they shot off while we hung back, laughing. We never planned to actually race them.

Eventually, Mom drove the Mustang too. In the early morning hours while we slept, she went to a twenty-four-hour laundromat to wash our clothes and the SuperAmerica gas station for milk and eggs, donuts and cigarettes. She once confessed to me she had to physically lift her numb right leg on and off the brake and accelerator pedals. I worried constantly after that, but she could not be stopped. With the Mustang, she could still be a mom, providing some nourishment and treats for her children and caring for our clothes and towels. Two years later when she had to get her license renewed, she hobbled into the Department of Motor Vehicles on my arm, without her walker, trying to hide her right-side paralysis. The clerk at the counter noticed it immediately, and Mom started to say she had sprained her ankle, but I cut her off and said, "She has multiple sclerosis." The clerk said my mom needed a doctor's letter saying she was fit to drive. Her doctor refused. She was mad at him for a bit, but got over it quickly, knowing he was right. Still, she continued to drive to get milk and bread at sunrise and go to the laundromat just like before, and I did not say a thing.

Mom got great joy from driving my car. It gave her some control over a life that had skidded out of control. Just like me, Mom knew the freedom of pulling away in that sleek and powerful vehicle from the hopeless mess of our yard and house. That car took me all the way through college and halfway through law school, and to nights of drinking and dancing in nearby Wisconsin, where the legal age for alcohol was eighteen instead of twenty-one in Minnesota. I burned out one engine and replaced it with a rebuilt one. I went from my first drink to blackouts. I rode home passed out in the back seat of my own car countless times while someone else drove. When they told me stories the next day about me dancing alone on the dance floor, or flirting with the guys at the bar, I could not believe it. Growing up, I vowed never to drink, but I'd quickly ended up an alcoholic like my father. Perhaps alcoholism is another thing my father gave me.

I never saw Dad sober except once for six months a few years before the divorce. I was about eight years old. For those six months, he came home right after work to have dinner with us. After my brothers ran outside to play, he and I stayed side-by-side in the cozy booth my mother installed in the kitchen, eating peppermint bonbon ice cream, his favorite, and suddenly mine too. It still is.

One night he did not show up. He never came home for dinner again after that. He kept drinking. The memory of sitting with him and eating our ice cream is the greatest memory I have of my father. That may be the best thing he ever gave me.

THE ART AND CRAFT OF PUBLIC ADMINISTRATION

WITH GENEROUS SCHOLARSHIPS, I WAS able to attend Hamline, a liberal arts university in St. Paul, an easy commute from our home, and majored in political science and French. In my third year I took a seminar in public administration. There were only fifteen students in the class and the professor arranged the long tables in a square so we could all see one another. Despite playing in the Al Anderson Combo, I was still shy to the point of phobia and hated this arrangement—there was nowhere to hide. I was about to drop the class when I saw our textbook, *The Craft of Public Administration*. It had a quilt design on the cover.

Back then, in 1975, it was highly unusual to use the feminine craft of quilting as a metaphor for public governance. I had not yet tried quilting, but I loved fabric and sewing. I sewed all my clothes on a treadle machine someone gave us until I could afford an electric one. This quilt image alone was enough to make me stay in the class.

The introduction to the textbook was equally compelling. The authors wrote that public administration has certain aspects that are scientific, but it is not a science; it has components that require artistry, but it is not an art. In the end they concluded it is a *craft*. The Craft of Public Administration.

Although I dreamed of being a professional musician and fine artist, I failed at both. Later on, I concluded I was *just* a crafts-person. This always seemed second-rate to me. Just making crafts was a hobby, not art. I made so many things growing up, but I never was complimented or appreciated for it by my mother or father. I could make just about anything, and I often made gifts to suit my family's unique desires: a hand-decorated vase for mom's roses, a custom-painted Green Bay Packers helmet for Mick. I even learned to sew a fluffy pink stuffed cat for Animal Town from a women's magazine. My dad's shirt cardboards from the drycleaners provided an endless supply of material, which I used to build an entire play kitchen in my closet, make poetry book covers and greeting cards, and use as canvases for my paint-ings. I typed the *Neighborhood News*, co-written with Mick—jokes, sports facts, and more—to hand out down the block. One entire summer, I alternated between sewing Barbie clothes on our back porch and building a wooden derby car in our garage out of the wood from our childhood sandbox.

When I started high school, our neighbor heard about my treadle machine and gave me a bolt of dull gray thin-wale cordu-roy she had in a closet. I had no money to buy cute fabric—we were terribly poor at that time, barely keeping the water, elec-tricity, and telephone in service. I sewed an A-line, V-neck tu-nic with large pockets and very wide-leg pants to wear to a high school dance. Even I was surprised by how stylish it looked. With a big-sleeved white blouse under the sleeveless V-neck tunic and a cheap long gold necklace, I was asked several times where I got my outfit. I wanted to be a fashion designer and drew clothing ideas constantly. When I had money from working at the diner, I bought expensive denim that looked like the American flag. It had wide red-and-white stripes and alternating blue stripes with stars. I sewed the coolest pair of jeans—hip-huggers with flared legs. I was wearing them one day, walking down our alley to the bus stop, when I heard a neighbor say loudly, so I would hear, "She sure dresses well for a welfare kid." I kept sewing, but I nev-er went down the alley again.

Because the authors of our textbook had such high regard for "craft," I decided to stay in the course, and I'm glad I did, because it was there I felt the stirring to work in the public service ranks.

On the last day of class, the professor decided to get me to join in the discussion, which until then I had mostly avoided. He asked the class if, after all we'd learned, did we think it was possible for a government agency to do anything of positive and lasting good for its citizens? Or was it just a bloated, overrated, and possibly corrupt political machine run by self-centered politicians for their own benefit? A couple of students spoke, and they were cynics, but they were clear and logical and made sense. Then he looked right at me and asked my opinion.

I felt my face turn red. He already knew my optimistic position from my assigned papers. I was an idealistic dreamer who wanted peace, not just in my home but also on earth. I never gave up on those dreams.

I stammered an answer. It was incoherent but I tried to say *Yes, this is possible. I believe that good can come from the government if the right people are in there.* I sensed everyone cringing and feeling sorry for me as I choked out those words. Or else they just thought I was naive, or both.

After class, the professor said to me, "Can you stop in my office? I have something I want to ask you."

I nodded and followed him, worried. He was not the kind of professor you would want to chat with. I sat in his small dark office and he looked at me.

"What do you plan to do after graduation?"

I blushed.

"Law school," I said.

I noticed his eyebrows twitch. He pushed his glasses up.

"Granted," he said, "you do 'A' work on your papers. But clearly you are very shy and I must tell you, you will never make it in law school, much less as a lawyer, with this problem."

I remember saying nothing, and as soon as I could escape, I

was out the door and on the way to my car, sobbing. I was dev-
astated. I knew it was true, but now he and the class knew it too.

I wished he had been like my beloved French professor, Dr.
Root, who saw my shortcomings and worked with me to solve
them. When I could not speak up in her classes, Dr. Root talked
to me about it. Kindly, privately, professionally. She remembered
that my scores on the entrance exam in French were remarkable. She knew I could read even difficult French texts with ease
and that I had excellent composition skills. She could sense that
I was always engaged in class and loved French literature and
culture. She asked what might be holding me back from being
able to speak French in her classes. I told her the truth about
my childhood, and my Mom, or at least the headline version. "I
understand," she said. "Your family situation is complex." This
was the first time anyone ever summarized my life in a way I
could accept. *Complex.* It was true, yet neutral. I liked it. I liked
her even more.

After that comment, she strongly recommended that I go to
France as an exchange student to get over my fear of speaking
French in class or anywhere for that matter. She handed me a
brochure, smiling. It was only for one month, our January interim
term, sophomore year. An entire month in Paris, living in a hotel in the Latin Quarter, studying theater, attending plays almost
nightly. She encouraged me to leave my mother at home for my
able brothers to care for while I lived in France. At first I was ap-
palled by her idea, then surprised, then excited.

French language and literature were my love and I wanted
to succeed. I had no money, but I asked our father's brother—
our intimidating Uncle John, the "rich lawyer uncle"—for some
money to cover the trip to France. There was a modest inheritance in trust for each of us children from Nana, my father's
mother. John was the trustee and had the power to dissolve the
trust to give us our money early. I requested he do just that. Nana
decreed in her will that it not be distributed until age twenty-five
in order to keep us on welfare (so Mom said) and to ensure Mom

did not get any benefit from it while we lived at home. Nana also wrote my Dad out of the will by giving him just one dollar (which the law requires to ensure you did not forget a child). Uncle John got everything. Fortunately he agreed with my request, "broke the goofy fiduciary" as he called it, and gave all three of us our money early.

I did exactly what Dr. Root recommended. I went to France for a month of theater study in Paris, then on my own initiative (and with the remaining inheritance) went right back the next year for spring semester, living with a family in Brittany. Our class traveled together to Normandy, La Loire, Chartres, and more. I fell in love with the high, jagged coastline and crashing waves of Brittany. On spring break, a friend and I hitchhiked down the eastern coast all the way to the Riviera and back without mishap. I was finally fluent. I never wanted to return to the USA.

Problems with my drinking followed me there. Being away from Mom for the first time in my life, I went a bit wild. I got drunk far too often and was behind on my term papers. At first, my French family thought I was a sweet, shy student, but they ended up disappointed and sometimes disgusted with me. The director called me to his office and warned me I was flunking out. I used worrying about my "crippled" mother as an excuse for why I drank so much, and told him I had only gotten As in French my entire time in college, which was true, but he was not moved by my tears. I panicked, thinking I would be sent home in shame with no credits. Luckily for me, he finally gave me another chance. I made a point to catch up on the schoolwork and go to classes, but I don't think I cut back much on drinking. After I knew I would make it through the semester, I called home and suggested to Mom that I stay on for the summer as an English tutor. She was adamant that I come home, saying there was no money and she needed my help, so I did. Before we hung up, she told me a plumber came and finally fixed the upstairs toilet—a "horrible project you are lucky to have missed," she said. I guess that was meant to sweeten the deal.

I wished this public administration professor had offered an idea on how to help me speak English instead of telling me I was a failure before I even began law school.

Despite his pronouncement, I did go to law school at night and took care of Mom during the day. Dr. Root was sad that I would not pursue an advanced degree in French, but she said nothing critical. I had high LSAT scores, and had graduated *magna cum laude* from Hamline with a double major in French and political science. From my application, no one at law school could tell I couldn't talk unless I was drinking.

I made it through law school with honors but never raised my hand. I suffered terribly during any mock trial or appellate argument. My trial professor said he could not focus on the merits of my case because he was worried I was going to pass out trying to present it. I remember exhibits shaking violently in my hand as I handed them to the court reporter. I wobbled in my low heels as I walked up to my professor, who was acting as judge, to submit the exhibits. I made no eye contact with anyone. My voice was shaky, too, and not loud enough.

Almost every night after class, around nine o'clock, I would go to a nearby pub with my new friends. Four women in the class who sat near me (we were alphabetized) became my closest friends for years. I told them most of my life story over drinks. I knew I drank more than they did, but they didn't judge me. In a few years, they would talk to me about my drinking problem, but for now, I think they saw me as a shy, smart, wounded person who loved to party at night.

Just two years out of law school I found out that my craftsperson self was my ally: I set up, advertised, and ran a solo law office, and built it into a successful family law practice. Next I worked for Legal Aid at their Native American Center, a creative and diverse community-based office. I found resources and proposed ideas to make things better for the clients, like adding a paralegal to the staff. Finally, after being appointed to the judiciary, I was able to create innovative court projects, including a personalized, human-centered family court and a traveling traffic court that went deep into the inner city to help restore driver licenses.

Dave did graduate work in chemistry; Mick earned a PhD in English. He is a novelist and poet, a beloved English professor and chair of his department. I am somewhere in the middle of their science and art. I see my place now not as a failed artist, but as a devoted craftsperson. No longer second best. Now I make small improvisational art quilts. I can usually make one in a day. This works well, not knowing how much time I have left. I always admired those anonymous Navajo women who made exquisite pottery to cook in and eat from that I saw in museums, and the poor Korean women who made bojagi wrapping cloths from little scraps of fabric they found and added each day. Bojagi now hang in museums, too, and look like modern art. Making something beautiful from whatever is at hand—and having the product be useful in ordinary life—is satisfying.

The cover of the textbook we used in my public administration class changed over the course of many reprintings. The quilt cover did not last long. Now the cover features a concrete public building with a large American flag draped near it. I dug deep online and after a lot of effort, found one used copy of the 1975 quilt cover edition for three dollars and ordered it. Holding it in my hands was powerful. I realized that many of my dreams came true. I could now speak, unafraid. I changed the family court process into a more peaceful and compassionate one. I did that by using creativity, life experiences, and even some art. It turned out I was able to change an adversarial institutional process into one that did some good.

The seeds of wanting to create a better legal institution were in me that day I was humiliated in class (and afterward by the professor), but I could not know that at the time.

After I retired because of the cancer recurrence, I found this quote from Thich Nhat Hanh, the revered Vietnamese Buddhist monk: *The practice of peace and reconciliation is one of the most vital and artistic of human actions.*

Long after I let go of any notion of being an "artist," his words brought this part of my life back to me. His quote helped me see that my work in the legal system was also artistic and creative. It was often more important than the law when working to resolve the problems of those who suffered.

Mom's Death

I STOOD BETWEEN MY TWO brothers in a navy polyester blazer and skirt, a white cotton blouse, and black pumps I bought the day before to wear to our mother's wake and funeral. Our neighbors, the Mortensens, were the first to arrive at the funeral parlor for the wake. They never had children and loved us like their own. In two years they would buy me a brand new Ford Pinto when my Mustang Fastback burned through its second engine. The Mortensens were hosting a gathering in their home following the funeral, providing all the food and beverages. They did what they could to comfort us. As she hugged me, Mrs. Mortensen pulled her red, white, and blue abstract silk scarf from her neck and tucked it in my open collar like an ascot. It looked much better on her ivory wool coat, and I thought it made me look like a flight attendant, but I had no energy to stop her.

Dave, twenty-five, stood on my left, and Mick, twenty-two, stood on my right. I had turned twenty-four just days before Mom died. We'd stood like this five years earlier at our dad's funeral. He'd been found dead in a downtown hotel room. We were told he had suffered a heart attack, but we knew it was the alcohol that killed him.

One evening in early August, Uncle John and his wife, Caroline, had knocked on our door. This had never happened before. Within minutes, Mom called all three of us to come downstairs. I was the first to walk into the living room.

Mom looked at me and said, "Ham is dead."

I hugged her and held onto her while she cried. I felt numb. After a few minutes, John and Caroline left with what might have been Dad's only remaining material possession, an older model luxury car, parked at the curb.

Alone in my room, in the hours and days that followed, I played Carole King's song "Tapestry" over and over again on my stereo. "The drifter in the torn and tattered coat" she sings about—that was Dad at my graduation. She seemed to summarize my father's life and death in a single line: "Once he reached for something golden, but his hand came down empty." I sobbed at the song's last line and still choke up when I hear it. "And I wept to see him suffer though I didn't know him well."

As people passed by with their condolences about our mother, we silently nodded at them. When Uncle John—my Dad's only living relative—passed by, looking and sounding as usual like Winston Churchill with wild eyebrows, pinstriped suit, gold watch tucked into a vest pocket over his protruding belly, he muttered in his affected English accent without looking at me, "Susan, report to Stan in my office Monday morning at nine a.m. for a job."

He was out the door before I could say anything. He was rumored to be extremely wealthy, making millions of dollars doing national class-action, antitrust suits. When our father failed to provide for us after the divorce, Uncle John came through with a used car, siding for our dilapidated house, and an occasional check. We were intimidated by him.

I had quit my waitress job sometime during college, and I took care of my mother during the day while attending my first year of law school at night. I had not thought ahead to what would fill my days now. We lived off monthly checks of a few hundred dollars, from my father's only asset, a life insurance policy that Uncle John had paid to keep in force.

After my mother died, I was not sure I could go back to law school. I was halfway through the second semester of my first year. In a state of shock, I was turning to alcohol every day for relief. My new boyfriend, Jake, and I would go to bars whenever we were together, and I started drinking at home, something I had not done while Mom was alive. Now that she was dead, I could quit law school and do what I really wanted to do: study French, or even just move to France. But I didn't. My girlfriends and Jake convinced me I had to go back to school a week after Mom's funeral.

For years after her divorce, she chain-smoked and was sedentary and overweight in addition to having MS. It was in August, right before I started law school, that Mom had a medical emergency. I heard her gasping for air on the couch and ran to her, but she could not communicate what was wrong. I called 911. She had not been to a doctor in more than ten years, despite our asking her to go. I was afraid she would be very angry when she realized I had called an ambulance.

Instead, she later thanked me for saving her life. The doctors told her it was a very close call, with congestive heart failure and blood clots in her lungs. She needed oxygen twenty-four hours a day and a handful of pills every morning.

When she came home in November, after three months as an inpatient in the hospital, she needed around-the-clock care. I knew then it was good that I was still there and not in France. No one told us that she was being sent home to die. In fact, before her discharge, the doctor told her, with me there, she needed to go into a residential nursing home. She smiled at him and said, "No. My Susie will take care of me." She grabbed for my hand.

I looked at the doctor, feeling panic, assuming he would tell her that was impossible. That she needed professional help. That I had just started law school. Instead he said, "Well, okay, then, Esther, if that is what you want." He left the room without looking at me.

I imagined what it would be like to take care of her for many years to come. The pills, oxygen, catheter, commode. I felt hopeless, but I could not contradict her. She told me many times that having us children was the only reason she could live with all the sadness and pain in her life.

"Susie," she often said when I was growing up, "you are my Rock of Gibraltar," and she repeated this again after the doctor left. I took over the grocery shopping around age twelve and pushed the cart home filled with bags of food, across several busy streets, and was mortified. With her encouragement, I learned to fill out her checks and sign them in her special signature. I could buy her cigarettes with a note at the neighborhood drugstore.

She seemed childlike after the hospital stay. Although I felt my world crumbling, I could not refuse her. I knew how sad she was in the life she ended up with—except for her children, she would be quick to add. Even so, I feared sacrificing the next ten or fifteen years of my life. I had no idea she would die just four months after she came home.

Back in 1979, we had nothing like hospice care, though I believe that is what she needed. Mick and I set up the dining room with an oxygen machine, a commode, dozens of bottles of medications, and an oxygen therapy device. We got insurance approval for a large mechanical recliner with a seat that moved upward with the touch of a button, to slowly boost her into a standing position, making it easier for me to pivot her from there to the commode. She did not want a hospital bed. Mom saw the chair on a television commercial while in the hospital, and since her doctor wrote a letter of support, it was covered by medical assistance (welfare). She lived in that chair.

Her legs were completely paralyzed. Her blood clots worsened and congestive heart failure was taking a toll. Her legs were so swollen I could not bear to look at them. Mick and I were with her all the time: He was with her at night while I went to classes, and I was with her during the day when he was at his college. Mick never criticized me for staying out after class drinking with my friends; he would just leave a note on how Mom was doing because I slept in after those nights out.

She hated the personal care attendants provided by medical assistance, but I liked them, because it meant I got a break. When they came, I gratefully rushed outside to have a cigarette. She told them to call me right back in. She wanted me to watch what they did when they were out of her sight. She thought they emptied her catheter in the kitchen sink instead of the toilet, which was just a few steps farther. They did not do that. I was tired and frustrated and burned out. I also felt important and special.

Mom's voice was nearly gone. She asked me for a wooden spoon from the kitchen drawer and I gave it to her. When I was upstairs or asleep on the living room couch, she would bang it slowly, over and over, on the metal tray next to her until I came. Sometimes I stomped down the stairs, annoyed, asking, "What do you want *now*?" I believed I would be taking care of her just like this for twenty more years. After she died a few weeks later, I was sorry and ashamed I talked to her like that. It didn't seem to matter to her; she just smiled when I entered the room.

I began sleeping next to her on an old sofa I dragged into the dining room from the back porch. I do not remember why I suddenly did this since the living room sofa where I'd been sleeping was in plain view of her chair in the dining room. As it turned out, I slept by her side every night when she entered the last weeks of her life.

Her only brother flew in from Nashville two days before her death. She had not seen him in years. Looking back, it seems he knew it was the end, even though I did not.

On her final day I awoke to a note on my pillow from Mick. It said she did not wake up when he came in to see her that morning at six, but she was still breathing normally.

I ran and checked, and she was still breathing, or so I thought. I called her name but she didn't answer. I crawled into her lap and hugged her, sobbing and screaming. I said, "I love you Mom," over and over. There was no response from her. I finally understood. I didn't want to move from there, but after a while I crawled out, called my aunt—her beloved younger sister—and told her what was happening. She calmly said I needed to call an ambulance.

I called 911. "My mom won't wake up!" I cried. "But I think she is still breathing!" They arrived minutes later with sirens on, but after they took her vitals, everything and everybody slowed down. I remember yelling at them, "*She's not dead!*"

They told me to follow them in my own car to the hospital. The ambulance had its lights on but the siren was off, and they did not speed.

The emergency room doctor finally came out. "We can keep her body alive on a ventilator, but all her systems have shut down," he said. "I am sorry, but they cannot be revived. It is up to you. I am so sorry."

I knew Mom got exactly what she wanted. She spent the last months of her life in the home she loved, with her children there. Even though there was no hope, I was not sure I could form the words to tell the doctor to take her off life support. It felt like a betrayal. But I must have said it, because that is what they did.

Our mother was pronounced dead shortly after that. A tiny nun came up to hug me, and I awkwardly bent down and sobbed on her shoulder. The cause of death on the certificate was a pulmonary embolism. I did not see her again.

Dave went to get Mick from school. They came to the hospital and I told them what had happened. They said that it was okay, it was her time. Dave left and took charge of arranging for her funeral and burial. I made sure he requested a closed casket. She would have wanted to be remembered as thin, young, and pretty, I thought. She never got over her weight gain or losing her glamorous looks from her youth. Though she'd spoken with people on the phone, no one had seen her in years.

For several years after her death, I had a recurring dream about her. I am looking out the front window, and there she is, coming up the walk to our front door, wearing her navy blue bandana scarf tied just under her chin to hide her dirty hair. Lumbering forward on her three-foot metal cane, her extra weight hidden in a baggy sweat suit, she looks happy to be home. The dream always seemed so real that when I woke up, it would take me a while to realize that she was not downstairs, that I'd never see my mother again.

III

HIRED

THE MONDAY AFTER MY MOTHER'S funeral, I showed up at my uncle's law firm in the same suit, blouse, and pumps, minus the scarf. Walking into Uncle John's offices was like walking into a palace, especially when compared to my home. Plush, handmade oriental rugs over hardwood oak floors, a huge reception area and offices, mahogany and leather furniture, grass-cloth wallpaper with gold threads running through it. There was even an entire lounge with a full bar, tables, and chairs, plus a sauna and shower. The entire top floor of the building was dedicated to John's office suite, with indoor, reserved parking just steps away from the entrance.

Stan, a business lawyer, had a smirk on his face during my interview. I was barely coherent from grief, a hangover, and my long-standing problem of shyness and social anxiety. Since Mom died, I was now drinking every day. Stan was the managing attorney and I was sure he saw me as a waste of money on their payroll, a pity hire, but my uncle, his senior partner and the business owner, had ordered him to do this. He offered me five dollars an hour, full-time, said it was way more than minimum wage, and I took it. I would be a gopher doing whatever the seven lawyers asked me to do, and I'd share a room with two other law clerks. I would go back to law school at night. My days and nights would be filled.

I sat there at my desk the first morning with no phone, a blank yellow legal pad, and a pen. No assignment, nothing to do. Maybe Stan had not yet told the other lawyers that I was there. The two law clerks in the room did not talk to me at all: They were in their last year of law school, and they just kept silently researching case law and taking notes. Just before noon, I gathered enough courage to go into Stan's office to ask for some work.

"Go to the file room," he said. "Learn the office from the bottom up. For now, just do what Anne says. She knows everything." He went back to writing on his legal pad while I still stood there, so I left.

Anne was about thirty, pretty, with a tiny frame, blue eyes, and long blond curls. Right away she seemed glad to see me and asked me all about myself. She seemed genuinely sad to hear about my mom's death and wiped away tears. She told me she had two young daughters in primary school, and her husband was a rising star of a trial attorney. Now that her girls were in school, she decided to work part-time. My second day with her, she brought the oversized family photos in the frames right off her living room mantel to show me. She also showed me the file system, which was in the same room with the coffee. When someone came in for a file or coffee, she cheerfully said hello to them by name, so I could learn who everyone was.

Every day I looked forward to our time in the file room. We had our deep conversations while we put away files or pulled them out. We abruptly stopped when people came in, which was often. That did not deter us. We picked up right where we left off. We covered childhood, school, dreams, and pain. I talked about my new boyfriend, Jake, and she told me about her marriage, with its highs and lows. Without her, I could not imagine being there. That new income allowed me to stay in my childhood home with Mick (Dave had moved out years earlier), get some decent clothes, and continue law school with some student loans. A few years into our friendship, we discovered it was her father who'd paid his legal fees to my father with the piano I loved so

much. That cemented everything. We felt our friendship was destined. It turned out that meeting her changed my life.

THE HAND OF AA

In those three years before I graduated from law school, Anne and I became best friends, and I was a regular at her family's dinner table. Anne was an extraordinary "down home" cook. I loved her two young daughters. They were funny, smart, active, and innocent. Anne was the kind and healthy mom I never had. The downside was that Paul, her husband, drank until he slurred every time I was there. Yet he was a "brilliant trial lawyer," just like people said about my father. It was a red flag, but I ignored it because I loved Anne and the girls so much. Paul looked handsome and successful in his Cadillac, and fine suits, with two beautiful, smart children and a brand-new home all by age thirty-five. They had everything I had for a short time in childhood and lost. I worried about them and hoped all would be well.

After a while, I became a part of the office drinking group. Uncle John had quit drinking years earlier, maybe when his younger brother, my father, died of alcoholism, but his law partner Morris drank. Morris was John's age, shorter but likewise squarely built, his hair as blond as John's was black. He was deferential to John in most things, a kind of legal sidekick: According to my mom, he played Barney Rubble to John's Fred Flintstone. But when it came to drinking, Morris was the mastermind. He encouraged me to drink more than I ever had in my life. He bought me my first-ever martinis. Morris and my uncle's secretary, Shari, seemed inseparable, even though both were married.

We three drank until the bars closed most nights. One morning he brought me a vodka and orange juice, which he called "the hair of the dog that bit you." I had never heard that before and laughed. It helped the horrific hangovers aspirin could not touch. I drank martinis with them every lunch and usually drank straight through the afternoon. It's hard to believe now as I look back, but no one from the office seemed to mind. At the fancy restaurant we frequented, The Blue Horse, our martinis were served in large tumblers normally used for Old Fashioneds, at Morris's request. We called them "buckets of martinis." We made sure to drink at least two on an empty stomach, before the Steak Diana or fresh walleye arrived, to get the full effect.

Morris drove us to the lunches in his white Lincoln Continental, and then to other bars. When they told me the next day of things I had done the night before—like taking flowers *and* the vase off a table as we walked out, then being grabbed and yelled at by the manager—my heart tightened as I realized I was having blackouts now almost every time I drank. I tried to cut back some, but never could.

One day we went back to the office late in the afternoon, which was rare, and, a short time later, I heard giggling turn into loud laughter. The entire office, except my uncle, was standing in front of my desk, and someone was holding a Polaroid photograph of me that they had just taken. It showed me out cold on my desk, sprawled over files, with my long hair covering my face. I felt ashamed to my core. I pretended to be amused, laughed along with them at the photograph, and knew I had turned the corner for the worse.

Morris knew my father had died of alcoholism; in fact he'd brought involuntary commitment proceedings against him several times for being a "public inebriate," as it was called back then. This forced Dad into the thirty-day inpatient treatments for alcoholism. After I was sober, I looked up Dad's commitments, which are public record. He had been committed fourteen times to inpatient treatment. Once he even went through Hazelden, the famous treatment center in Minnesota, and I was told by one of his friends—who thought this was hilarious—that my dad stopped at a bar on his way back to the city, where they gave you a free drink in exchange for your thirty-day sobriety medallion. Morris and I never mentioned my father.

In addition to being a daily drinker, from morning until closing time, I was now smoking more than two packs of cigarettes a day. I'd been introduced to cocaine, LSD, and mushrooms, which I tried once or twice, but my preference was always for alcohol.

Jake and I fought a lot when I was drunk. He sometimes locked me out or left me in random places without a way home. We had no cell phones back then and I was terrified in addition to being drunk. Jake seemed to find me repulsive at those times, and I was crushed the next day when I realized he still did not want me. I went begging for him to take me back, which he did, but not right away. I'd suffer for a week while he partied with his buddies. He would call, apologize, and I'd forgive him. This pattern continued even as we planned our wedding. My closest friend from law school confronted me and said she refused to stand up for me in my wedding because of his abuse. Feeling lost, I called his mother, who had welcomed me like a daughter into the family. I told her how Jake treated me. She said I didn't deserve that and should end it immediately. I knew she was right but still I stayed with him.

I was able to graduate from law school a semester early, in December, by taking summer courses. I wanted to get out of there as soon as possible. The bar exam was three months later, in March, and after I passed, I was sworn in as a lawyer in May. My uncle hired me as an associate attorney.

A few weeks after I graduated, Anne's husband, Paul, surprised me by showing up at my office unannounced to tell me he had quit drinking and wanted me to know he was concerned about *my* drinking.

"Well, that's great for you, Paul," I said, trying to sound enthusiastic, and then I lied and said I had a client waiting. I rushed him out.

On St. Patrick's Day, a few weeks after I took the bar exam and was awaiting the result, my uncle's office held its annual open bar for lawyers and judges and anyone else who wandered in after the annual parade. This year, Shari had the idea to order green-and-white baseball jerseys with the firm's name and "Drinking Team" printed on the front and our name and a number on the back. She made a few extras for the people we drank with regularly. She and I started drinking at about ten a.m., and by noon the office was shoulder-to-shoulder with lawyers, judges, and friends of the firm. At some point that evening, I ended up in a suburb forty minutes away in a hotel room with a sixty-year-old attorney from Texas who practiced antitrust law with my uncle. It seems I passed out before anything physical happened, and when I woke up to his snoring, I felt complete disgust and slipped out of the room. As I made my way through the lobby, I noticed his young associate watching me from the bar. I found my car in the parking lot, drove the wrong way on a major freeway, got off, and got lost a few more times. Somehow I made it home, and I woke up a few hours later, on my back, vomiting all over myself. I was aware I could have died of asphyxiation like Jimi Hendrix, a guitar idol of mine.

The next morning I was cleaning up, going through my wallet to see if I had lost anything, and I saw the "Ask and Ye Shall Receive" card my friend Carol from the diner had given me years before. Just then the telephone rang. It was the associate. He sternly told me that I was going to end up losing everything, my reputation and maybe my life, if I did not stop drinking. I thanked him and hung up.

I looked at the holy card. I asked Jesus, God, or anybody to help me. From that day forward, I vowed every morning not to drink, but I still ended up drunk every night. I took the ten-question quiz that was in the newspaper one day, and it shocked me to realize I was already an alcoholic.

Somewhere around this time—those weeks remain a sad and frightening blur—while drunk and hopeless after one of those fights with Jake, I wanted to die. I floored the accelerator of my Pinto as I approached a massive concrete barrier on Highway 94. At the very last second, I turned the wheel away.

Finally, in late July, I called Paul, drunk and crying, asking him for help. He left his youngest daughter's birthday party on a Sunday afternoon to meet me at a diner in St. Paul. It was a favorite hangout for sober folks. He brought me the book *Alcoholics Anonymous*—the "Big Book" as it is commonly called. I had been drinking as usual, before I showed up. I remember trying multiple times to get my yellow Pinto into a parking spot and kept driving up the curb. People could see this from inside the diner, but Paul was not there yet. I was glad for that.

I don't remember any of the words he said to me, just his passion for the program and his joy that I called him for help. Paul was possibly the smartest man I had ever met and I idolized him as a lawyer. If he endorsed AA, I would try it. We agreed to meet outside his favorite AA club the next evening. I agreed not to drink until then.

I stayed up all night reading the Big Book he gave me. No expert treatise on alcoholism could have held my complete attention or moved me like the personal stories of suffering and recovery in that book. Their stories could have been my own.

The next day just before noon I saw Morris on his way to my office to get me, assuming I was going with him and the usual group that drank to oblivion every afternoon. I grabbed the phone quickly as I saw him coming and pretended to be on an important call, covered the mouthpiece and whispered loudly, "Go ahead without me—I have to take this call." As soon as the partner left, I called Paul in a panic and his secretary put me right through. I dreaded calling Paul because he was so busy and important, but I knew I had to. I didn't know how I could make it through the day without drinking. I told him they were waiting for me at the bar and restaurant next door. He was short and to the point. "Stay away from them," he said. "Do not drink. Call again if you need to. Meet me outside of the meeting house at five o'clock." He sounded like he was busy, yet he still made time for me.

I counted the hours remaining. The office was calm now because most of the staff was next door and would not be back. I remembered the Big Book in my briefcase. I got up and locked my door, sat on the sofa, and read it all afternoon. If you could make it through one day, they say you can make it through an entire lifetime. One day at a time.

The meeting house was a spacious and charming old mansion. It also happened to be just a block from where I went to law school. I couldn't believe this place was here the whole time. I parked on the street outside and slumped down in my Pinto, waiting, sweating, dreading the next steps. I was tempted to drive off. Just then Paul pulled up in his Cadillac and parked in their lot. I was filled with shame walking up the steps with him in the blazing July sunlight. I told Paul I was afraid someone I knew would see me. "You're not ashamed to stumble out of the bars downtown at three o'clock in the afternoon," he said. "So why would you be ashamed to walk into a place where everyone is sober?"

I smiled weakly and crossed the threshold.

The greeter smiled broadly and shook my hand. "Can you handle a hug?" he asked. I nodded. Others in the front room who were chatting before the meeting smiled at me and said, "Welcome." They offered me a cup of coffee and showed me to our meeting room on the main floor with a large table in the middle. I whispered to Paul that I needed to sit next to him and he nodded. We took our places around the table, about a dozen of us. In the brief silence before the meeting began, I knew this could be the first chapter in my new life.

What no one knew yet was that as I came through the door, besides having to face and accept my problem, I also felt despair, realizing I was like my father—which was unbearable. I vowed never to drink, yet here I was. I felt like a complete failure at twenty-seven.

As the meeting progressed, something struck me. Everyone here spoke humbly, as fellow human beings and not as psychologists, teachers, doctors, or lawyers. In fact, many of these professionals were there (especially the lawyers), but no one shared that out loud. The principles of the program were what mattered. The focus of AA is on sharing personal stories of "experience, strength, and hope"—not expert opinions. The only requirement for membership according to the Big Book is "the desire to stop drinking." I did not have to label myself, not even as an alcoholic, which made it possible for me to go in the door that day. I said simply, "My name is Sue and I have a desire to stop drinking." That desire and a brand new law degree was all I had going for me that day, July 22, 1982. Somehow, after that day, I never had to drink again.

For someone like me with an extreme social phobia, the meetings provided a safe space to practice talking without alcohol. There were kind and compassionate folks who knew just what I was going through because they had all been in my shoes. In our small circles I could have said "pass" whenever it came around to my turn, but I vowed to try to say something every meeting, and I did. I usually brooded over what I said afterward, hating it, and could not hear the other people's words after that.

Next, I learned to be in an intimate and trusting one-to-one friendship with Audrey, my sponsor, someone I could call day or night instead of drinking. I could tell her anything. Later, when I was stronger, I was told (not asked) to speak to recovering addicts and alcoholics at the county detox inpatient units, and next at large AA gatherings that filled auditoriums. I was scared and shaky each time, but the program said we need to carry the message to those who are still suffering. It is one of the basic principles. This helped me take the focus off of me and look at the needs of others.

Several of my new friends would always go with me. Before my first talk, they made it very simple. There are three parts, they told me. Just tell them what it was like, what happened, and what it's like now. I allotted fifteen minutes per part and filled up the time easily. I could have kept on, but I watched the clock and kept to the plan. Receiving a roomful of applause, then dozens of hugs over cake and coffee afterward for telling my story of failure was something I can never forget. It helped others stay clean and sober to hear my story. It helped me to tell it and to be welcomed unconditionally again just like at my first meeting.

After a few years, I was able to speak comfortably with others, meet new people, and do even more public speaking. I definitely would not be considered shy by my AA friends anymore. Once I started trusting and talking, I kept going. I knew Mom would have been overjoyed that I finally got over that painful obstacle. Even though some might judge her as a neglectful mother, I knew in my heart she wanted us to be healthy and happy. She did encourage us to get excellent educations and we knew she loved us. We also received the love of her parents, my beloved grandparents Theresa and Ewald.

Several things stand out to me that made all the difference on that fateful day I asked for help. First, the "hand of AA" was there when I reached out. Next, the people in AA welcomed me with dignity and unconditional acceptance without knowing who I was or what I had done. The program is based on a fellowship of human beings who all have the same problem, and because of that, there is no judgment. If there had been, I could not have returned.

I went in the door of AA that first day to stop drinking, which I did, but the fellowship also taught me how to live. I diligently went through each of the twelve steps and did whatever my sponsor and the Big Book told me to do. I even went to a "fifth-step hearer" (a nun at a twelve-step treatment center) and told her everything I wrote in my fourth step, every defect and transgression and every bit of harm I could remember causing. I did the daily inventory at night (Step Ten) and tried to catch my negative behaviors right away. When I got to the final two steps that talk about prayer and meditation, I bought the book *How to Meditate* and read mystics like Thomas Merton and Simone Weil. It is possible that what motivated me most of all were the "Promises of the Program," which every member knew began on page eighty-three of the Big Book. They told me I should read it morning and night when I was feeling down or hopeless:

> If we are painstaking about this phase of our development, we will be amazed before we are half way through. We are going to know a new freedom and a new happiness. We will not regret the past nor wish to shut the door on it. We will comprehend the word serenity and we will know peace. No matter how far down the scale we have gone, we will see how our experience can benefit others. That feeling of uselessness and self-pity will disappear. We will lose interest in selfish things and gain interest in our fellows. Self-seeking will slip away. Our whole attitude and outlook upon life will change. Fear of people and of economic insecurity will leave us. We will intuitively know how to handle situations which used to baffle us. We will suddenly realize that God is doing for us what we could not do for ourselves.

I was still not ready to say there was a God, but I certainly knew I gained some power from the group, the teachings, and my sponsor that I never had before. That would be my higher power. My favorite promise was: "We will intuitively know how to handle situations that used to baffle us." I yearned to have that ability instead of floundering around not knowing what to say or do most of the time.

When I first volunteered to be the greeter about three years in, I stood at the door and welcomed newcomers to their first meeting. They looked shaky and afraid. I imagined seeing myself through their eyes: a sober, healthy woman, smiling, offering hugs, showing them the way to the coffee and the meeting room.

Don't Make a Federal Case Out of It

I WAS FINALLY A REAL lawyer. A few months sober, working the principles of the program. While most of the office still drank, I attended meetings at noon, at night, and on the weekends.

Stan called me into his office to give me one of my first court hearings—a federal case. As he handed me the file, he explained there was a motion to compel discovery against our client, a Chicago construction company. The hearing would be in a month. "You need to write the opposing brief and argue the case in federal court," Stan said. "Can you handle that?"

Whenever Stan called me into his office, I felt like he used the opportunity to intimidate and mock me. When he'd heard I got my law degree *cum laude,* he'd said, "How'd you pull that off?" For three years he saw me disappear for my three- and four-hour lunches with Morris and Shari and just shook his head in disgust. This was my chance to show him what I could do.

I walked back to my office carrying the file in my arms like a new mother with her baby. I quickly opened it up and was surprised how little paperwork was inside. There was a motion from the opposing side and a few pieces of correspondence hiring our firm. That was it.

Our client, a large construction company based in Chicago, was accused of faulty construction, design, and materials because a building's foundation was cracking. They were also being sued for submitting inflated invoices for work and materials.

As I read the opposing side's brief, I thought, Oh God, our client is guilty of negligence and fraud. There's no defense here. He gave me a loser file to humiliate me in federal court. Our client should have just handed over the documents, but I didn't care to argue with him. I sat down to write and nothing came. So I set up the form: the header, the introduction, the conclusion, and the signature line. That's all I could do after one entire day.

I studied the rules and could find no defense for not turning over these documents. In addition to the documents, the opposing side was seeking a thousand dollars in attorneys' fees for having to bring this to court. I decided I had to call the lawyer in Chicago, our co-counsel, to see if I was missing something.

I was afraid to call him. I'm sure I picked up the phone and put it down a number of times before I dialed. It was one of my anxious habits. I asked for him and thankfully he wasn't in, but I left a message. Back then I was still smoking at my desk (thinking at the time I would never give *that* up, but I did a few years later). I smoked and worried and thought about what I should ask him. What I really wanted to say was, "Why didn't you give them the documents?" But I didn't dare. My uncle had already taken a sizable retainer. I had to do this, I thought.

Just then I got a call back. I began shaking when I heard his name announced over the intercom. I picked up the phone. "Hello, Jeff, this is Sue Cochrane," I said. "I'll be handling your case at the hearing next month. Just had a question or two."

"Who are you?" he asked. "We hired John Cochrane because he supposedly is the best fighter in the country."

"I am his niece," I explained. "I've worked here over four years." (Only three months as an attorney but I did not say that.) "The managing attorney asked me to handle this motion. My uncle must be out of the country that day—which he often is."

"Why can't you get the hearing continued until he gets back?"

"The managing partner said we needed to show up, so I assume he tried."

"Well, all right. Why did you call me?"

I froze, then stammered an answer. "I'm working on the brief and wondered what the reason was for not supplying the documents, or at least some of them," I said. "They do seem as though they could lead to relevant evidence. I guess there's something I don't know here. I hoped you would fill me in."

"There's nothing to know," he said, clearly annoyed. "This is a highly burdensome discovery request. This was a multi-million dollar job. They chose our client's company to design this building and put it up. Our client is a respected national construction company. To get all the time records from hundreds of workers from two different states, plus invoices from every contractor and subcontractor, would take years. The rules only give us thirty days. Even if we had twice that, it would be impossible. Some independent contractors can no longer be located. They used proper specs and high quality materials and these guys are just trying to get out of paying our client's bill. Do you understand?"

"I see," I said. "Thank you. I just wanted to have all the facts before I wrote this and submitted this to court."

"We told that all to your uncle months ago. I'm still upset he is not handling it. It is simple and you should win hands down."

We hung up. I felt even worse. It seemed like even if what he said was true, the other side had a right to see the records, especially if the building was cracking and sagging. At the very least, it would exonerate the company. Now I had a buzzword to go on: "burdensome." That is a valid objection in certain cases. I wrote an extremely short brief in response, saying that these requests were burdensome. I repeated that several times. It was all I had. I got to the part requesting a thousand dollars in attorneys' fees and had no idea what to say.

I took a deep breath and went down the hall to see Morris, my uncle's partner—the one who used to take me drinking for those "five-martini lunches," and who brought me screwdrivers in the morning. Since I got sober, everyone who drank in that office gave me the cold shoulder, including him. After I quit going out with them to drink, I wasn't getting my phone messages and thought that was on purpose. So I sent out a memo to all the secretaries saying I wasn't getting my messages and asked politely that they be sure to put them in my slot. I said I would come up and get them. (After I got sober, Morris gave me a different office, all alone on the ground floor under construction, which struck me as punitive. It was noisy and smelly, and the construction fumes seemed toxic.) Morris had gathered up all the memos I had placed on their chairs (this was before e-mail) and threw them on my desk right in front of me, his face red, and said, "Who are you to accuse people around here of not doing their job? I'm their boss, not you. Just do your job."

I'd avoided him after that until this moment. With trepidation, I went upstairs and all the way down the long hall to his office. I went in and sat down. He looked up with no expression or welcome. I gave him a brief description of the case and I told him it looked like it was going to go against us—but I would fight, I added—and they've asked for a thousand dollars in fees. I told him I wrote a brief but I didn't think we were going to win. The Chicago attorney for our client thought it was a slam dunk. I asked him what I should do about the attorneys' fees.

"So these are Chicago lawyers?" Morris said. "They all fight aggressively and sometimes dirty. Just say it's a frivolous motion and ask for the same amount in return. The judge will cancel it out and nobody will get anything."

As I walked down the long hall again, I was proud of myself for facing him sober and glad I had gotten an answer. But my heart pounded because I did not find anything about this motion to be frivolous. I dropped the word frivolous and simply typed that our office sought a thousand dollars in fees to defend the motion. Later, I would bcome used to representing clients in their divorces when opposing counsels asked for sums of money over the moon, just hoping they would get half. I would never agree with that strategy and I hated myself for using it now.

I had a long road ahead of me to learn how to face this conflict of knowing the truth but being unable to speak it out loud. I was sober only a few months, and the program demands "rigorous honesty." I could be honest with myself much of the time but froze inside when it came time to tell others the truth. Especially if they were angry men.

The evening before the hearing, I could barely sleep. I got up and put on my one and only navy blue suit, which I still had from my mother's funeral. I added a blue-and-white pin-striped oxford blouse and a new pair of navy pumps.

I parked my Pinto across from the Minneapolis federal courthouse and went in. My anxiety ratcheted up. I walked up to the stately marble circle, where two kind-looking, gray-haired ladies sat giving out information. They directed me to the courtroom floor. I started shaking on the way up in the elevator. Even my teeth were chattering as they did when I was extremely nervous. The sound of my heels clicking on the marble floor made me want to hide.

I've never felt so alone, I thought. The absence of my parents for the rest of my life struck me hard at that moment. I wished I had just one parent. No parent saw me graduate from law school. There would be no parents at my wedding or to see my children, if I ever reached those milestones. I wished my mom and dad were there to see me argue my first case in federal court. Or just to say "Good luck." Anything.

I pulled on a huge golden handle to open the door to the courtroom. A massive bench, marble and mahogany everywhere, flags and gold, with sky-high ceilings. And, in front of us all, high above everyone, was the judge.

I tiptoed toward the chairs in the back of the court room, which was jammed with lawyers and clients and files. I dreaded having an audience.

One by one, the cases were called. Now I prayed I would be

last and no one would see this. Then the bailiff called our case, and it was my turn. The back of the room was still full.

I sat all alone on my side of the massive counsel table, because our client was in Chicago. The attorneys for the building owners sat across from me. They were hired from the metropolitan area's largest and most respected law firm. Both attorneys were tall, slim, tanned men, with perfectly groomed hair.

They smiled at me while they reached across and shook my sweaty hand before the judge reappeared.

"Where's John?" one asked. "We expected him to come in and pound the table." I looked confused.

"You don't know John's famous advice? He tells new lawyers that if you don't have the law, pound the facts. If you don't have the facts, pound the law. And if you don't have either the law or the facts—pound the table!" They laughed. "He's well known for that."

I knew now why they did not send John. We did not have the law or the facts or anything on our side. They would pound on me.

I wished I could say exactly what I thought at that moment: *Tell us what you need and let's resolve this. We want to correct this.*

The bailiff cracked the gavel. As the deputy shouted "All rise!" my heart sank.

They argued their side and I realized that my gut instinct was right all along. They had the law *and* the facts. When they finished, the judge swiveled briskly from them to me and looked right at me and said, "Miss Cochrane. What do you have to say?"

He locked his fingers together and put his hands under his chin, like he was about to witness something extraordinary. I stood up and softly said a few sentences about the production requests being burdensome and the client objecting to them. Then I sat down. He stared at me for what seemed like an eternity with those hands under his chin. The whole room went silent. Suddenly he slapped both hands loudly on his bench and said slowly and clearly, "Miss Cochrane, do you really believe your services today are worth one thousand dollars?" Someone in the audience chortled.

I stood up again, as slowly as I could. I felt every eye in the courtroom burning on me. I could see in my peripheral vision the attorneys at the table trying to hide smiles with their hands. I briefly imagined going off on a tirade, completely in French, then storming out. Or just silently walking out.

I had signed and filed an affidavit swearing under oath that one thousand dollars was the amount of fees it took to prepare that flimsy brief and to appear today for this ten-minute hearing. Morris had steered me wrong. His directions led to the ditch on the side of the road.

Uncle John had taken their five-thousand-dollar retainer, then left on an African safari, leaving me to "get valuable experience."

I paused. Everyone, even the court reporter, fingers poised in the air above a keyboard, was staring at me. I knew that if I said *no*, I did not put that amount of time into the case, then I could be charged with perjury for lying under oath on the affidavit. If I did that, I could be disbarred. For a moment, it seemed like the best plan. If I said *yes*, that my services were worth that amount, I would be a laughingstock.

"Yes," I said softly.

"Well, you are wrong!" exclaimed the judge, slapping his hands once again on the bench, the timing coinciding exactly with the word *wrong*.

"If your client does not allow these attorneys to go through all the files starting next week, until such time as they are satisfied, I will charge your law firm and your clients one hundred dollars per day until they do," he said, pausing after each syllable. "Do you understand?"

I nodded and sat down. I had never felt my face hotter or redder than it was at that moment. I walked out with my head down before the other two attorneys got up. I tried not to run, tried not to cry until I got to my car. Some tears started falling as soon as

I stepped outside the building. I ran across Third Street, got into my car, and sobbed on the steering wheel.

A saying I heard in AA says, "Everyone we meet teaches us something. Some teach us what *to* do, and others teach us what *not* to do." I learned a lot that day. I learned that I knew a bad case when I saw one. I learned to listen to my inner warning system. I learned that I could be set up and even humiliated and could still survive.

I turned on the radio to calm myself before driving on the freeway back to St. Paul.

Billy Joel was on my regular FM station, singing, "*You had to be a big —shot— dintcha . . .*"

That made me sob some more. I had been puffed-up over having this federal case and had a long way to fall.

I wanted to drink, quite badly, but knew this was not worth losing my brand new, hard-won sobriety. I may have been humiliated, but I was sober. I have no memory of relating the decision to the Chicago attorney and that is just as well.

Twenty years later, I would be in that same courtroom again. Not as a lawyer but up on the bench presiding over family court cases. The federal court built an all-new modern courthouse a block down the street, and our family court, previously crammed on one floor of the old courthouse, got this building for our own. The Family Justice Center. They gutted all but the main floor and left the marble information circle on the main floor. They installed all new, state-of-the art courtrooms with huge chambers for each judge. My courtroom had a spectacular wall of windows behind the counsel table. My view from the bench was of the historic mill district and the riverfront. I was randomly assigned to a coveted corner chambers, with windows to the ceiling on two walls.

That court appearance was locked away in my darkest reservoir of shame, and I hadn't realized when we moved in that this was the same building, even though I knew it was "the old federal court house."

Twenty years after that first hearing, clipboard in hand, I studied the main floor of our family courthouse, preparing to submit a proposal to revamp the entire entry system. I wanted to create an inclusive environment where the court welcomes each person that comes in and offers them immediate, respectful, and personalized assistance. I even used the Apple store as a model in one of my talks, but I pictured comfortable chairs and art, not stainless steel and glass.

I leaned against the marble circle with my clipboard to observe the people coming in. Passing through the metal detector. Searching for information or signs. It was then I remembered. I remembered the two women seated in the circle at the center of the main floor, who helped me find the courtroom. On this day it held sheriffs' deputies, who watch all the courtrooms on closed circuit television, ready to attend to problems if needed.

I relived for a moment the younger version of myself from twenty years before. I was not all-new and improved like the courthouse, far from it. But that federal judge I faced twenty years before helped to shape my judicial demeanor even though I did not realize it until now. He taught me what not to do, ever. He taught me to be truthful. He taught me to never yell in court. That judge also taught me to be especially kind to sincere, shaky young lawyers making mistakes in front of lots of people.

Matthew Good Elk

AFTER WORKING FOR MY UNCLE as a sober lawyer for two years, I left and opened my own law practice with money we got from selling Mom's home. (I also bought a brand new navy blue sports car with that money, with maybe an unconscious desire for that Mustang Dad gave me.) Then I was recruited and joined an elite family law firm located in a glass tower downtown. That lasted only six months, and I quit without another job lined up. I did not enjoy the wealthy clients fighting over money in their divorces, and I missed being my own boss.

I planned to go back to my former solo law office when I saw an ad for a legal aid attorney in St. Paul. I had applied for a position there right after I graduated from law school, but Reagan's massive budget cuts to legal aid forced a hiring freeze and the position was cancelled. I became a monthly volunteer instead, at the main downtown St. Paul Legal Aid office. I liked the people there and the office environment. The staff was friendly and appreciative whenever I took a volunteer case.

I was excited to read the ad, which described the position as a "community-based legal aid attorney" stationed inside the St. Paul Native American Center. Few Native American clients came to the downtown office, so Legal Aid collaborated with the Native American Center to rent a small office inside their community center.

The job required being able to manage an office, and if possible, experience with the Indian Child Welfare Act. I applied quickly, then began studying the Indian Child Welfare Act. I read everything—the statutes, the rules, regulations, and cases. After several interviews, I got the job, and because the pay cut was significant, I sold my sports car and bought a small cheap one.

The new law office was tiny. The Native American Center was located on University Avenue near downtown St. Paul and the State Capitol, a major thoroughfare. Formerly it had a streetcar; now it had a bus that went all the way to Minneapolis. This was the main route most of our clients used to get to the center. They came for food, services, coffee, community: Members of over 140 nations, all living in this urban area, visited our center.

This was back when University Avenue had no improvements, no light rail system. I could see women in super short cut-offs leaning into car windows to talk to men who pulled over, then getting in and driving away. The city bus rattled my front window every twenty minutes. I closed the blinds.

I received clients from the food shelf next door, or the foster care program across the hall, or by word-of-mouth. It started slowly but grew quickly. I was welcomed and included in all community activities: I went to powwows and fry-bread taco days, and even was blessed by a spiritual elder who visited us one day from a distant reservation. He spoke rapidly in his own language but the words "staff person" were loud and clear when he paused to bless my head in the circle as he went around behind us. I played on the center's softball team, had friends, loved my work. Due to the increase in clients, I got a budget for a paralegal and a summer law clerk.

My first week there, with blinds closed, I heard tapping on the outside wall, and then my telephone intercom announced that Matthew Good Elk was in the lobby. My supervisor had briefed me. He was in his sixties, blind, with poverty-level disability payments each month through the SSI program. The attorneys who preceded me in this position had a case in federal court that they'd kept postponing until they found an expert witness for their rather odd theory for his case. Until the trial occurred, he just stopped in to check on it. Every day, I soon found out.

He received very little on his monthly disability check and lived in a run-down high-rise housing project downtown, well known for violence and drugs. He had a caregiver who came three times a week, tidied his apartment, made sure he had food. Cut his thick steel-gray hair in a short, chopped-off manner. He lived on frozen dinners that he microwaved. He told me later that everyone assumed he'd been blinded by disease (I wondered that too) but it occurred when he was riding his horse at eight years old on the Rosebud Sioux Reservation; an accident with some branches on a tree caused him to lose his eyes. His lids never opened and were slightly sunken.

The tapping became a daily ritual. If I was with a client, he waited silently in the lobby. He would be sitting up straight, hands on his cane, when I came out. I would gently say, "Hello Matthew, it's Sue," and he would put out an arm, which I met with mine. He would walk into my office on my arm, without using the cane.

He spoke very few words but always pulled out mail for me to read to him—almost always junk mail. I offered to throw it away but he refused and took it back home. Every year he received a check of about two thousand dollars from grazing fees on the reservation. He had no choice over the Bureau of Indian Affairs renting the land out to ranchers for cattle to graze. Receiving the check counted as "earned income" and disqualified him for the next five months of his disability payment. This seemed unfair, and clearly there needed to be an exemption from this penalty for disabled Native Americans. He struggled to pay utilities, food, and other bills, and he would put many bills off until the grazing check came.

The previous attorneys had discovered a real estate principle, called *fructus naturales*, that could solve the problem. *Fructus naturales* was simply a Latin phrase for "natural fruits" of the earth: trees, shrubbery, grass, natural growths. Things that do not need cultivation by humans. Thus, when they sent Matthew money for "grazing fees," this was, we argued, a sale or rental of *real estate* (grass), and should not be counted against him because money from selling real estate did not count as income. It was a strange law and theory, but it made sense. And it was all we had.

I wrote the University of Minnesota Law School and the chair of the real estate department asking if they might analyze this theory, and, if they agreed, would they testify *pro bono* (no charge) for a poverty-stricken, elderly, blind Native American living in an urban housing project. They sent back an enthusiastic yes. The professor wrote a detailed letter, and agreed we were correct, and we were ready for trial in federal administrative court.

Right after that letter came, I got a call from an attorney out west. She said she'd heard we had a case pending regarding the issue of seeking exemption for grazing fees. I told her yes, and she asked if our client was able to travel with me to Washington, D.C., to testify before the Senate Select Committee on Indian Affairs. There was a bill proposed to make these fees exempt.

I checked with Matthew and he agreed. I talked to his doctor, too, with his permission. We received the date and time. Legal Aid put up some money for his flight and lodging, and Matthew's former pastor in South Dakota sent a matching check for food, airfare, and clothes.

The more I prepared for this hearing, the more I envisioned Matthew testifying in his own language, his own voice. I knew several people who were fluent in Lakota and contacted one of them. She agreed to come along as an interpreter, and I found enough extra money somewhere to get her airfare, and she and I shared a hotel room.

By this time, over a year into the job, Matthew was part of my daily life. Every day I heard the tapping and looked forward to seeing him. Same thing, every day. Led him back to my office on my arm. Walked him to the bus, his left arm on my right arm, his long elegant hand lightly touching me. I never told Matthew that one day I was coming out of our downtown office after a team meeting, rushing to lunch, and I suddenly saw him, moving faster than anyone else down the busy sidewalk, swinging his cane expertly and moving gracefully through the crowd. I watched him for a good block, saw him cross a street, continuing at a quick pace. His "need" to hold my arm was not a need at all. Maybe I started it, with my ignorance, I do not know. But he never corrected me. I smiled at our mutual secret many times.

All was not that smooth. He had a problem of incontinence. Often his mail was soaked and smelly. If I could not read it, I silently disposed of it. I learned to place a towel on his chair. I wished someone would help him with this. Before we left for D.C., I asked his doctor if there was a medication that could help Matthew. All he said was "adult diapers." It was so hard for me have this conversation with Matthew but I bought them, he packed them, and he wore them. He was clean and dry the entire trip. After we got home, he quit wearing them, even though I said they were free if he wanted more. He refused.

We made it through sweltering heat to the hotel in D.C. I had bought a lightweight black suit with a rayon ivory tank top. I had to spend part of my apartment rent money to get this simple suit, but it was a wise choice as it turned out. Elegant and cool. I slipped the silky blazer on just as we got to the Senate office building.

The day before the hearing, we explored the city. The interpreter, a woman in her fifties, and I took Matthew to the Vietnam Memorial, where he touched the wall with us; the Washington Monument; and the Lincoln Memorial. Hearing her describe these sites and read their inscriptions to him in Lakota made my heart fill with joy and also sadness for all he had lost in life.

When the interpreter needed a rest, I took Matthew to tour the White House, and I described everything to him. I knew he enjoyed that—the coolness, the quiet, and getting to hold my arm for hours.

Suddenly we were surrounded by the Secret Service. I was so busy looking at the walls and ceilings and architecture, I'd missed

a "Do Not Enter" sign. I explained we were here to testify at a
Senate hearing tomorrow. This was before 9/11 and they just led
us away. I explained to him what had happened, and he smiled
a rare smile.

That night we ate at a famous restaurant beloved by senators and journalists, where Matthew ordered a steak and sent it
back—twice—for tasting "funny." I was embarrassed but thankfully they were gracious and did not even charge us. We found
a convenience store, got him a microwave dinner, and cooked it
at the hotel. In the middle of the night, he knocked on our hotel
room door, the adjoining room, needing some kind of help. It
was an anxiety reaction, I thought. He was so courageous to leave
his familiar life to do all this. I told him how many Native Americans like himself he was helping and that by noon the next day,
we would be done. I realized we had done too much on our first
day and went back to bed.

The next day, the day of the hearing, I had a page of questions
all ready. We practiced once in the hotel, my questions in English,
translated by the interpreter, his responses in Lakota. Listening to
him, I felt my heart almost breaking. I had never heard him speak
in Lakota before, other than a few words when I asked him how
to say thank you or hello. It was such a magnificent language,
and it offered both a connection and a contrast to his life today.
It allowed him to take the lead. If I had done it the usual way, I
would have asked leading, yes-or-no questions. He would have sat
there like a human exhibit. I am glad I listened to my intuition.

The Senate hearing room was unlike anything I had seen.
Beyond the grand federal courtrooms or the State Capitol in
Minnesota. A huge marble sculpture of a Native American man
leaning back on a horse with a bow-and-arrow pointed skyward,
greeted us in the lobby. We were called in. Many of the senators
were already seated, high up, in curved rows. I knew several of
them from the news by name and photograph. Inouye, Daschle.
Right before we started, our senator from Minnesota, Paul Wellstone, came running in with his aides. He climbed to his seat and

smiled down at us. Wellstone was a staunch supporter of the organization I worked for—he had been a volunteer there himself, in southern Minnesota, before being elected to the Senate. I had met him a few times and was impressed he made it to this hearing—I never told anyone in D.C. we were coming.

Matthew spoke. My questions were quiet and simple. The interpreter and I sat off to the side, and Matthew was in front facing the senators. He sat straight in his chair, wearing his new plaid, short-sleeved shirt and black pants. Speaking Lakota, his voice was deep and clear, perhaps amplified by the marble floors. The room seemed completely still, yet electric. I felt tears forming, witnessing his juxtaposition of poverty and dignity. I hoped the senators were moved by his presence the way I was. Matthew never lost his composure. I noticed a group of reporters gathering in the corner. I was shivering a bit from the cool cathedral-like room and the anxiety of facing a Senate committee.

Then it was over. Wellstone rushed down to thank me and to shake Matthew's hand. Matthew turned to him and said, "Are you Daschle?" Matthew was born and raised on the Rosebud reservation in South Dakota, where Senator Tom Daschle was known as a champion for Native American causes.

"No," Wellstone told Matthew. "Sorry. I will get him for you." And he did. While Matthew talked to Senator Daschle, I gave an interview to an Associated Press reporter and others, after which an article appeared in a major newspaper and was picked up by our local press. I never read it but our executive director told me how good it was and how happy he was that we did this.

Other senators and staff then gathered around Matthew to meet him, thank him, shake his hand. I watched from the edge and was grateful beyond words that he was at the center of all of it. Suddenly, we were ushered out and on our way home.

Life went on. The case in federal administrative court was scheduled soon after our trip. We had no idea if or when the bill might pass. We had to go through with the trial. Our expert witness was a young real estate professor of law, who was well prepared and articulate. Matthew testified, again with his interpreter. But the judge was inexplicably hostile. He berated me and kept referring to my *cause célèbre* in D.C. I was aghast. I had never been treated with such anger and disrespect in a court of law. But I kept going. I have no idea why he treated us like that.

I came out of the courtroom and burst into tears. The expert witness hugged me and patted my shoulder as I sobbed and apologized. She admitted she could not believe how brutal the judge had been and complimented me for presenting a strong and good case. We were both sure he would rule against my client. He did. (His law clerk, a Native American man, made a subtle apology when I called the office with a procedural question about the court order a few weeks later. I said nothing. It still stung.)

Appealing meant years of litigation in federal court. It could end up in the United States Supreme Court. Matthew agreed to let lawyers in other states do that, since we would certainly all benefit if they won. Thankfully, after our testimony and others' in Washington, D.C., the Senate Select Committee on Indian Affairs voted to provide the exemption that grazing fees would not count as income and disqualify Native Americans from receiving their poverty-level disability payments. A victory. A good law. Matthew lived to know he helped Native Americans everywhere.

After seven years I left Legal Aid to join the family court bench. It was hard to leave the center but I hoped to reach even more people in crisis in my new job. A few months into my family court position, someone called to tell me Matthew had died. I still miss him.

WHY DID GOD ABANDON US?

I HAD ASKED THIS QUESTION of myself many, many times. Now I would ask someone at Loyola, a place where one can receive "spiritual direction." I had tried therapy, almost seven years of it. I went every week to see a psychologist who had helped my AA sponsor, Audrey, during her chemical dependency treatment. The therapy was not covered by insurance and this was difficult on my Legal Aid salary, but I knew I needed it. At one point I was in group and individual therapy every week. Still, I was unhappy. I read spiritual writers like Merton and Weil, studied the AA Big Book, and practiced all of the twelve steps of AA, but still I could not find relief. I looked forward to something I had not yet tried.

I waited in the lobby to meet my personal spiritual director, Liz. The pamphlet I received in the mail said this was an opportunity for me to talk about my life in an intimate way—my relationships, my career, my hopes and worries as well as my challenges and joys. Unlike therapy, where we look for a treatment to solve a mental health problem (in my case it was probably trauma and depression), the focus in spiritual direction is finding the sources of meaning and purpose in our life, which could be God, our higher self, our soul, our work, or even our family or community. There was no pressure to believe in any religion or set of beliefs. This was a refreshing idea after those years of rigid Catholic education from kindergarten through high school graduation.

Liz brought me back to her office, where I sat in a comfortable armchair. She was a nun, dressed in lay clothing, with a delicate sterling crucifix at her neck. Within ten minutes I was crying, as I usually did when telling a new person the secret stories of my childhood. I guessed she was about fifty, with clear blue eyes, soft skin, and short white hair. I envied her appearance of serenity even while I sobbed.

I was thirty-five years old, single, renting an apartment in Minneapolis near the Rose Gardens of Lake Harriet. I enjoyed being a lawyer at Legal Aid, but I was convinced I could never own a house, buy a new car or new clothes, or travel because my salary barely paid the rent, food, and gas. I also wanted a loving, permanent relationship and possibly children. I could adopt a baby as a single person if I had the money, but after seeing my mother struggle all alone, I knew I never would.

My relationship with Jake had ended when I stopped drinking, and I grieved for several years; we were planning to get married, I had bought a wedding dress, and Uncle John was going to provide a reception at his country club. I wished Jake would call and say he was sober and sorry and that we should start again. I drove by his house late at night sometimes.

I met Clair in our first semester of law school. We were not in the same section, but met in the student center where my new girlfriends and I played cribbage before class. He shyly approached our roundtable and joined us to play one afternoon. We all became good friends, and he came with us when we went to our favorite pub. I knew he was interested in dating me, but I had fallen hard for Jake at that time. Clair and I became close friends, sharing our grief when his father died soon after my mother had. When Jake and I had one of our fights, Clair would ask me out, but I only wanted Jake. Clair patiently waited until our final break-up. I tried to be in a relationship with him then, but it was too soon for me, plus now he lived and worked in a small town an hour north of the Twin Cities, and neither of us wanted to move or leave our jobs. Then he met someone new and was in a serious relationship and I was alone again.

After almost a year of sobriety, one of the men, Aaron, from my noon-hour group, started asking me out for coffee, first with the group. After a few weeks, he invited me to dinner at a new French restaurant. He was older than me, divorced, with an eight-year-old daughter. He had at least five years of sobriety when we met, and he seemed like a kind person. At dinner he disclosed that he was breaking the rules to ask out a "newcomer" and could be accused of being a "thirteenth-stepper." I knew that rule, and although I was not initially attracted to him, I felt my ego rise up and said, "I know what I am doing. I have a law degree."

We continued dating, and I learned his family owned a very old and successful business in the city. He was a delivery person, had not gone to college, and did not like to read books. I wondered how this could ever work out, but I was swept away by his joy of living sober, his constant effort to ensure my happiness, his gracious family, and his complete lack of worries about money.

When I opened my law firm, he was there every step of the way, helping me move, then serving papers for me and delivering supplies. Soon he bought a two-bedroom condo minutes from my office, and we moved in together; he gave me the underground heated parking spot and proposed marriage. I accepted the heirloom emerald-cut diamond in a modern wide band as my engagement ring. As time went on, I missed being able to talk about books and poetry, since we shared none of that. Having fun, eating out, taking trips were not enough. I ended the engagement after I went to Legal Aid, and he was angry and threatened to put my possessions on the street if I did not return the ring that day. Legally it was a gift and I could keep it, but I returned it. I cared about his family and worried they would also be upset about me ending the engagement. I went to different AA meetings and never encountered him again. His mother wrote me a card that said I was "a beautiful thread in the tapestry of their life."

My sponsor, Audrey, was married when we met, and soon she and her husband, Ken, adopted two babies from Korea. I became a second mother to them, as Audrey put it. I was at the airport when her children arrived from Korea about one year apart, and I loved them more than I ever expected to. I devoted my vacations, spare time, and scarce funds to her children for five years. I loved sewing clothes for them, especially elaborate Halloween costumes. Audrey and Ken took several weeks a year to travel to New Mexico for art and writing retreats, so I would live in their home, drive their van, and take on all the responsibilities of a parent. I felt exhausted afterward but also proud of myself.

Audrey told me once that if I ever felt taken for granted I should tell her. One time I did try to tell her about my pain— wanting my own children, my own husband, my own home. That I also needed time alone, space, and to not be so heavily counted upon by her family. It was a given I would travel with them on every vacation and virtually every weekend outing. She once confided to me that their decision to adopt a second child was based in large part on me being in their lives.

She looked shocked as soon as I started to express my feelings. She thought that I was saying I wanted out of the whole friendship, which would result in my abandoning her children. Seeing her panic, I retracted everything. Once she realized I wasn't ending anything, she said with a smile, "If you don't have your own children, you will have had all this time with mine. If you do, you will be *so* experienced!" She looked satisfied, as if she'd fixed everything.

The truth was, I did need more solitude, but I could not say so. Audrey had become my best friend, but I was also intimidated by her. Maybe because when I met her at my second AA meeting, she had four years of sobriety and I had four days. She walked up to me and said she would be my sponsor, so I agreed. I idealized her, without meaning to. From that day on I was immersed in the AA life and wanted to please her.

As the years went by, I did not have what most single people treasure: freedom of movement, independence, and spontaneity. And my favorite thing—after working with people all day: unobserved time. Once I cancelled a weekend up north with Audrey and her family in order to meet a boyfriend's mother in Iowa, and she was angry. That relationship did not last long because he drank too much, but I also knew Audrey did not support me being with him.

At Loyola, I told Liz all of this. I told her of my childhood. The violence I'd witnessed and my mother's collapse into despair. After what happened, I carried a secret belief into adulthood that I had paid my dues, gotten more pain and suffering than most do by the age of twenty-four, and that my life would be happy from then on. After I was sober, I was in pain again, and it did not seem fair.

The longer I talked while Liz listened, the more I felt I was getting somewhere. I looked forward to our monthly sessions. She listened and asked questions that caused me to look inside for answers. She took my pain seriously.

I told her about being raised Catholic. As a young child I believed in Jesus, God, and all the saints. I even felt I had spiritual or mystical experiences in church, during singing, praying, or reading about Jesus. I felt my heart open when I learned that Jesus' unconditional love fostered kindness to all people—lepers, robbers, prostitutes, murderers. I wanted to be like him, maybe even be a nun. Catholic grade school in the 1950s and early '60s was not a time for feminists—the nuns said that women could either be mothers or nuns. As a child I was leaning toward nun, with good reason, given what I had already seen modeled at home.

I was taught Jesus was kind and loving and God was all powerful. So how could they let what happened to us happen? My father was a raging alcoholic who beat my mother in our presence. I saw him drag her by her hair down the hallway while she screamed for him to stop. He smashed and broke the dinner plates against the wall if he did not like what she made. All three bedroom doors' panels were kicked in because she locked herself in to get away from him. Sometimes we crouched with her in the dark corner of a closet, praying he would leave and not find us.

Dad never physically hit or touched me, but he verbally demeaned and sexualized me, which confused me. I was ashamed of my body before I started kindergarten. He was obsessed with my legs, how long they were, and wanted me to show them off. "Susie is put together well," I heard him tell a neighbor, when I was in a bathing suit running through the sprinkler. One night, I was about four years old, bathed and fresh, wearing a silky pink nightgown with lace and a matching robe that Grandma gave me for Christmas. Mom got a phone call that he was coming home, I overheard that and was thrilled. I got out of bed, feeling pretty, and sat at the top of the staircase above the entry where Dad would come in. He walked in, looked at me, and said, "You better damn well learn to keep your legs together." I felt dirty.

He could be cruel. We all heard him yell to Mom, as he walked out for the last time, "I hope you die and soon and in a wheelchair." We ran to hug her as he slammed the door.

Mom's sister, Marie, brought us groceries after the divorce because Mom was too proud to file for welfare. Finally, she did, but drove far away to shop so no one could see her using food stamps. Mom didn't go to college, but after graduating from high school, she won a statewide competition for her speed and accuracy in shorthand and typing, which landed her an executive secretary position at a well-known publishing company in St. Paul. She was very smart, but she had been out of the job market since she married, over ten years. And even if she could find a job now, she could not use her hands, which were numb from MS.

Dave, Mick, and I started missing school almost every week. When the head nun and principal of our grade school called and said we had the highest absenteeism of all the students, Mom said, "Call me back when they stop getting all As," and hung up on her. She bragged about doing that. Sometimes we missed school because Dad's break-ins kept us awake most of the night. Many times we could not find our school uniforms in the messy house. Or we couldn't get out the door on time. Possibly we just couldn't get out of bed.

Mom quit cooking, but she could still drive. She escaped from the mess and pain in our house by driving us around. We called those outings "Happy Hops." We ate fast food up and down busy Robert Street in West St. Paul. We did our best to hide the destruction and chaos from everyone. Other than our maternal grandparents who took the bus to our house nearly every day to help Mom in the months after the divorce, we did not let anyone into the house. Once, however, Mom had to let in a child protection worker.

I do not know who reported her. She called me into the living room, with no notice, to play my guitar for the worker. I was eleven years old or so, and I did it, with a red shame-filled face. I hated hearing her being funny and smart with him. Even flirtatious. She assured him we were all right and she would get some help around the house to clean it up. The abuser, our dad, was gone. Her children were on the honor rolls, straight As. She handed him a page torn from the community news that listed our names and academic achievements. He left and never returned.

A few years before that, my mother had been crushed to find out that according to the church, she should not divorce her violent husband. The pastor apparently mentioned the word "excommunication." The day she talked to him, I found her crouched on the bottom step, sobbing with the black dial phone in her lap. She explained what excommunication meant. "They're kicking me out. I can't have Communion again."

That is when I started doubting the existence of God—around age nine. "I'm quitting the Church too if they don't want you," I told her.

My dad wasn't even a Catholic, but he'd pretended to be just so Mom would date him and agree to marry him. She found out a few weeks before her wedding that he was an atheist. Before that, he not only went to mass with her every Sunday, he even took Communion. A priest allowed the wedding to take place in

the St. Paul Cathedral (where I also had my high school graduation ceremony) but in a dark side chapel—not at the main altar
which she had dreamed of.

Dad agreed to raise us Catholic, signed an official document,
and that settled it. He never went to church again. Before I graduated from high school, I considered myself an atheist too. I began to drink even though I swore it off as a child because of Dad.
I was unhappy, drank even more, and joked that alcohol was
cheaper than a psychiatrist. I feared men. Although I had a few
short relationships, I had to be drunk to be intimate with them.

After I got sober, no matter how much therapy I underwent
or how many meetings I attended or how many self-help books I
read, I was still in pain and haunted by that question:

Why did God abandon us?

I tried churches: St. Joan of Arc, a liberal Catholic Church;
Unity (all about *love*); and the First Universalist Society. I turned
to books looking for the answer: poets, spiritual writers, mystics,
and philosophers. Thomas Merton, Henri Nouwen, Frederick
Buechner, Carl Jung, William James, Simone Weil, Rainer Maria
Rilke. I found comfort in their words when reading them, but still
the pain was with me.

One of the AA daily meditations said, "God does not save
a drowning man just to throw him into deeper water." At first
after I sobered up, I clung to that like a life raft. Now, eight years
later, I thought I was the exception. I would soon drown, alone. I
would hint about my misery in AA meetings and they always said,
"You're sober today. Be grateful. Go to extra meetings. Help another alcoholic." Some days that made me want to punch them.

It took until about the fifth or sixth session for me to ask Liz
about the reason I was there.

The time came. I asked her, "Why did God abandon us?"

"God did not abandon you." She paused. "Your father did."
She said this quietly, with assurance.

"I can tell you were loved," she said. "You were unconditionally loved by *someone*—or else you could not be who you are—kind, generous, thoughtful. Who might that have been?"

I immediately realized who had loved me unconditionally all through childhood: Mick, of course. His unconditional love and admiration and sweetness were always with me. When we lived in our family home after Mom's death, he was deeply saddened by my drinking and my abusive boyfriend. He never rejected me but silently carried the grief of what I was doing. After I sobered up, he told me he once saw me and a group of drunken lawyers stagger out of a bar downtown in the bright sun at three o'clock in the afternoon on a summer day. He was on his way to apply to be a Big Brother. The morning after my first AA meeting, he was joyful and supportive and never faltered.

In the world of adults, it was my maternal grandmother, Theresa, who embodied unconditional love. She seemed to live the teachings of Jesus to love one another.

When my father was on his violent drunken rampages, my grandmother took care of me and Mick. I always rushed into her house to hug her ample body, her cheeks red from baking, gardening, canning, and making soap. Our grandparents had created a small farm on their inner-city back lot, and we ate the tomatoes, carrots, potatoes, and green beans at our meals soon after we gathered them. They'd raised my mother and three other children during the Great Depression with hard work and unfailing faith in Jesus. Every night on their back porch, we said the rosary and every Sunday went to Mass. After church, I would swing under the grape arbor on the wooden swing Grandpa made, kicking higher and higher, watching Grandpa catch Mick's pitching. Then we'd settle in at the round oak table in Grandma's kitchen. We would watch her bake and cook while we ate warm apple pie or her crinkled molasses cookies. We never said much, but I basked in the warmth of her loving presence. Grandpa showed us how to use his carpentry tools—he was self-taught and could make anything people asked of him. Mick and I spent hours in the basement workshop where we would go "pound"—that's what we called hammering nails into boards, at first just for fun. As we got older, we learned to saw and made a birdhouse and helped make benches.

When Mom was dying in our dining room, which was set up as a hospital room, I remember her calling out for her mother, our grandma, who had died a year earlier, in 1978. My mother had her mother's name as her middle name: Esther Theresa Cochrane. I chose it for my confirmation name, Susan Marie Theresa Cochrane.

"Theresa!" my mother called several times, a few hours apart. Her voice was loud and clear and joyful, even though at all other times it was a raspy whisper. I was stunned. She raised her arms weakly, trying to reach out to her mother. It appeared as if Theresa were right in front of her. Mom died two days later. I hoped Mom saw her mother, Theresa, who welcomed her with her unconditional love.

I ended my sessions with Liz a few weeks after that, finally feeling a sense of completion. My interest in a spiritual life deepened, especially the importance of living a life showing love to others. I happened to sit next to Liz at an event thirty years later, and I overheard her introduce herself to someone. I hadn't recognized her. I tapped her shoulder and told her how powerfully her words had affected my life.

In the next four years, my relationship with Clair deepened. We mutually realized we wanted to get married and have a family, if we still could at our age. Even though he loved his condo on the lake north of the city, he sold it and changed jobs so we could live together in Minneapolis. We married in a small civil ceremony and within a few years bought a charming older home in Minneapolis near Minnehaha Creek. We adopted three baby boys from Korea, and I was appointed to my dream job on the family court bench, where I could reach many more families every year who were in need. The pay and benefits were four times that of Legal Aid, making it possible to afford three international adoptions in two years. I'd never thought when I was young that

I would go from "welfare kid" to making six figures. Even when cancer struck when the boys were so young, I did not collapse into despair like my mom did. It was undeniably hard, especially when I thought of the boys losing another mother, but I never reverted to that place where I felt totally abandoned. I had Audrey (we'd stayed friends), my brothers, many friends and colleagues. I also needed and found support through the holistic healing offered where I got my cancer treatment.

When I learned two years later that the cancer may have metastasized to my ovaries and I needed surgery, I went to the Commonweal Cancer Help Program in California founded by Michael Lerner and Dr. Rachel Remen. I'd read their books, and I knew I had to go to their retreat center, located on the Pacific cliffs in Bolinas. This passage, in Remen's *Kitchen Table Wisdom*, quoting psychotherapist Carl Rogers, inspired me to do better in my relationships and with those I saw in court:

> Before every session I take a moment to remember my humanity. . . . There is no experience that this man has that I cannot share with him, no fear that I cannot understand, no suffering that I cannot care about, because I too am human. No matter how deep his wound, he does not need to be ashamed in front of me. I too am vulnerable. And because of this, *I am enough*. Whatever his story, he no longer needs to be alone with it. This is what will allow his healing to begin.

THE BOOK OF ESTHER

IN HER LAST YEARS, MY mother seemed to live on the surface of life. With good reason—after Dad left, she needed to focus her limited energy on survival. Food, heat, housing. I would criticize her frequently in my own mind (and sometimes to her face) for not being a deep thinker anymore. I tried to read to her while she was trapped in her chair, crippled, but she wanted none of it.

She was not always like this.

My earliest memories seem too idyllic, too dreamy, like the 8mm color silent movies Dad and Mom took every holiday that captured only smiling faces, abundant dinners, and over-the-top decorations. No fighting, violence, or alcohol. We had times of joy and creativity, but they didn't last long.

Mom went all out on birthdays, Christmas, Easter, and Thanksgiving. For Christmas, she decorated our home with her handmade table centerpieces and door hangings made from fresh holly—she had to have both solid green and variegated varieties, with the red berries, too—nestled into pungent evergreen branches, which she brought in by the armload and piled in the front hallway. Our living room smelled like a forest. To her centerpieces, Mom added oversized bows she made from gold ribbon, then pine cones, and gold ornament globes. The branches of our living room Christmas tree were covered with the same handmade bows. Mom added strings of lights to the tree, making everything glow. Then she strung lights and fresh evergreens around the large mirror above the sofa as well. She did not stop there. She went outside, got up on a ladder, and nailed fresh evergreen branches across the eaves of the entire front of our home and around the front door frame, then added lights on top of that. Mom even put a second Christmas tree, fully decorated, in our remodeled basement "recreation room."

For the holiday dinners, the dining room table was set with her Franciscan china, the pattern of deep maroon apples and brown branches winding around the edges, the same set her mother had. All family members who lived in town sat around that table with the five of us: Grandma and Grandpa (Mom's parents) and her older sister, Marie: single, in her thirties, smart and beautiful, the first public health nurse in St. Paul. She spoke fluent German and played piano, and my middle name came from her. She had a girlfriend named Betty for years, who seemed like her intimate partner, and most likely was. Marie dressed in slim suits, nylons, and pumps. One Christmas she left her tall fur hat on all evening, and I petted it whenever I walked past her. Later in life she was disabled physically and mentally, and her erratic behavior frightened us. Our grandparents took care of her in their home until they died.

Uncle John, Dad's older brother, was at the table, also still single in his thirties. He was short and portly with a bulldog face, and he filled his plate two or three times. Dad and John's mother, our Nana, was there, dressed in a nubby wool suit and matching pillbox hat with the veil pinned up. She was a small woman, stooped over a cane when she walked in with Uncle John. She sat at the end of the table opposite Dad. She was color-blind and so was my father. Nana could draw, paint, and sew—her thread, fabric, and paint all labeled to indicate their colors. Her pencil sketches of baseball players in action, sliding into home plate or kicking up a leg to pitch a fastball, taken from the daily sports page, made me admire her, even though she was stiff and formal around us. Someone mentioned to her that I wrote poetry and liked word puzzles and spelling, and she immediately quizzed me to see if I knew the meaning of the word "erudite." I was scared of her.

Nana was one of the rare women of her generation to have a college degree, and she worked as an English teacher after her husband, a railroad executive, died young at the railroad where he worked. Dad was six years old when his father died. No one ever spoke of Dad's father, or of his brother David, who committed suicide. When we were young, we were told that David was a conscientious objector to World War II. Later, we heard other versions of why he hanged himself. We have one sepia photograph of him as a young man. He looks thin, sensitive, and more handsome than his two brothers. That is our only memento, other than the fact that Dad insisted his first son be named David. When I met friends and colleagues of Dad's while practicing law in St. Paul, they told me that Dad was the one who found his brother hanging, and that is when he became an alcoholic at age sixteen and quit going to high school. Dad lied on his admission form to law school and later bragged he was the only lawyer without a high school diploma. The deaths of his father and brother scarred him. Even though he caused us so much pain, he too suffered.

During the holiday meal, Mom constantly moved back and forth from the kitchen to the dining room, leaning over the table with serving platters, her apron tied over a silky dress and pearls. We had standing rib roast and mashed potatoes for Christmas, roast leg of lamb with mint jelly for Easter—the only time Mom liked her name because people said "Happy Easter, Esther!" For our birthdays we could choose our favorite main course and dessert, and the entire group would gather once again.

Mom was not much of a baker, unlike her mother, but once a year we had a special Christmas dessert she made and we could barely wait for it. I watched her make it (it involved no baking, just chocolate wafers and whipped cream). It took hours to set while the wafers plumped up with cream. I loved the black and white stripes that emerged when she cut the cream-covered log on the diagonal. We also had vanilla ice cream, and we could drizzle crème de menthe or crème de cacao over it. I may have had an early propensity for alcohol because I remember licking the spoon and the bowl and asking for more. I favored the crème de cacao. No one seemed to care how much I had.

Before these holiday dinners, I stood at the front windows waiting for Grandma, Grandpa, and Marie to arrive, especially on Christmas. We had received piles of presents from Santa that morning and were excited to show Grandma and Grandpa our favorites.

All summer, Mom was focused on our yard and the gardens she created. I remember her saying she planted "bent grass" in our yard instead of the bluegrass everyone else had, because it was soft on bare feet. It felt like silk to walk on. I discovered years later when I learned to golf that the putting greens are made of bent grass. Each year a pile of black dirt was delivered in our alley behind the garage, and by herself she spread this over the entire lawn, front and back. The lawn was buried in black dirt and I thought she ruined it. She told me not to worry, and soon the grass came through, thin at first, then thicker and softer than before.

Just after sunrise, Mom would be somewhere in the yard, cutting curved borders with an old butcher knife, dusting and pruning her roses, planting new flowers and shrubs. Grandpa took the bus over frequently to work on the house—he painted trim, repaired holes in window screens, and patched cracks in the backyard steps.

We had a huge Haralson apple tree at the bottom of the hill on one side of the yard. Mom asked Grandpa to help her cut the hill back to make a natural stone retaining wall. She planted a mix of ivy and wild flowers that grew between the stones. Then they dug up the rest of the lawn on that side and laid patio tiles. For the finale, she asked him to build her a wide, wooden circular bench around the tree. He did exactly that. Grandpa could build anything, from his own garage to a birdhouse and our bike rack. He could also fix most anything, without training or education.

The patio, shaded by the apple tree, turned out to be my favorite spot; it's where we put my sandbox that held the soft white sand Mom and Dad gathered from the caves by the river. A mass of orange poppies bobbed in the breeze on top of the retaining wall, and hydrangea bushes with giant white flowers leaned in to fill the entire shady back corner. The poppies were stunning and no one else had them. One summer day Mom came home with a birdbath and put it in the center of the upper garden, with the poppies gently encircling it. She then placed a concrete goddess statute on top. The goddess was meditating with her eyes closed and had on a tall pointed hat. This was one of those moments, and there were many, when I was in awe of my mother's creative ability and her courage to try new things.

When Mom worked in the gardens, she wore cut-offs and an old white shirt of Dad's and always had bare feet. At the end of the afternoon, she would lie in the hammock to work on her tan, smoking a long Benson and Hedges cigarette. Every week Mom would bring in an armful of jumbled flowers and greens, plop them on the kitchen table, and begin arranging them in a vase. I was surprised by her final arrangements. Each time she would start with a tall branch or flower in the middle that I thought was far too big for the vase, but when she was done, it was lovely. I use her method to this day.

Her gardens attracted people driving or walking past our house, who stopped and asked to walk through the yard and learn more. Even so, she still created a fun-filled child's paradise on the other grassy half with a high quality swing set and slide, a large above-ground swimming pool, and a "merry-go-round" that one day appeared. I am not sure what to call it—there were four green seats, and each seat had yellow bars for hands and feet. They were all attached in the center. When we pumped the bars with our hands and feet, the entire mechanism went around and around so fast that we leaned back and screamed. I have only seen a similar ride at a carnival once. Needless to say, the neighborhood children preferred our yard to any other, and Mom worked silently in the flower beds while we played. She was known to bring out pitchers of Kool-Aid and sandwiches and cookies when we least expected it.

The cracks in this beautiful life appeared when Dad was drunk at night. He drank Fleischmann's whiskey at home on weekends. He would often yell and throw things, and it was my job in the summer to run around and shut the windows so the neighbors could not hear him.

My picturesque life was also fractured when someone close to the family began to molest me. It started when I was about seven years old—with him fondling me and exposing himself. I told Mom this person "scared me," but I was unable to tell her what exactly happened. She said she would be watchful, but I still felt terror whenever the person was near. The abuse finally stopped in my early teens, but the impact was permanent.

When Mick and I were older, we had the Animal Town club-house to escape to: The upstairs of our two-car, two-story garage was like a large attic with double windows on two sides, and we arranged old furniture up there. I was the president of Animal Town. I made membership cards and we voted new people in. Mick (the vice president) and I never mentioned the talking stuffed animals to the neighborhood kids. This Animal Town was for helping real animals—we put on a carnival one summer and made eighteen dollars and donated it to the Humane Society. We handed out flyers offering to walk or bathe the neighbors' dogs but got no takers. I started a musical trio that performed door-to-door and we got donations or cookies. I sold Christmas cards I ordered from the back of a comic book, and without telling Mom, made bouquets from her garden and sold those too, for a nickel or so.

Mom and Dad had a social life for a few years, and they rarely hired a babysitter because we could sleep over at Grandma's, but when they did, an elderly woman named Mrs. Beaulieu came over. While Mom was getting ready, I sat on their bed watching her in the dressing table mirror, putting on her makeup, twisting her long hair into a bun, and spraying on her perfume—Chanel No. 5. When she walked out the door in high heels, she looked glamorous to me—even her lipstick matched her nail polish—with no trace of the barefoot gardener with dirt under her nails.

Mom and Dad had occasional outdoor barbecues for his friends and their wives. They served drinks and martinis made at Dad's new bar downstairs in the remodeled rec room. For her birthday one year, he bought Mom a large electric rotisserie, which used a motor to turn the meat over a fire. Mom made her famous blackened barbecued chicken with it. She taught me her secret marinade recipe: orange juice and Western dressing. Occasionally a piece of chicken fell from the rotating spit into the ash and coals, which she quickly dusted off and claimed that made it even better. She enjoyed entertaining. Mom told us that at one of their parties, a local newspaper columnist, George Eckersley, came up to her and said, "I hear from everyone how funny you are. Say something funny." Without a pause or a smile, Mom looked back at him and said, "George Eckersley."

I also saw when things did not go so well, like the time Dad threw a whole watermelon down the basement steps shortly before the guests arrived. I have no idea why he did that. Mom was about to carve the shell into a handled, scalloped basket that she would pile with fruits and melon balls of all shapes and colors, spilling like a cornucopia onto a silver service tray. They must have had a fight about it, or maybe he was already drunk. Somehow Dad ended up cleaning every bit off the steps, and it was the only time I saw him looking remorseful. She served a fruit tray instead, interspersed with sturdy sprigs of fresh mint from her garden.

Inside our house Mom had fine furniture and draperies with coordinating carpet. She created her personal version of the mid-century modern home, mixing fabrics, leather, and wood. When we were asleep and they had guests over, she would bring them up to our bedrooms to show us off, I suppose. We had round, room-sized hooked wool rugs that had large modern patterns and were soft and thick enough to play on all day. Having the prettiest home must have been important to Mom; I remember our clothesline had the first patterned sheets in the neighborhood— stripes for Dave and Mick, flowers for me, and solid burgundy colors for Mom and Dad.

Mom made our birthdays special, cooking our favorite foods and desserts by request and taping a poem to the wall next to our birthday breakfast place setting. It always started out with: *Roses are red, Violets are blue* and ended with something like, *Special birthday wishes to my special daughter Sue.* If I ever doubted my mother's love for me, I could recall the birthday where she rearranged and redecorated my bedroom while I slept. I was obsessed with ballerinas for a time and awoke to a set of three Degas prints spread across one wall, each with a different ballet dancer. My bed, with me in it, had been moved in front of a sunny window. A new white, mirrored dressing table, with movable side mirrors, now stood across from the bed. On top of the dresser was a hand mirror with a matching brush and comb set, all decorated in silver with red roses. A small white wicker chair completed the lovely vignette. When I was older, I refinished it in other colors from time to time. I could not let it go until we were selling the house about five years after Mom died.

When we were toddlers, she read literature to us: poetry and stories from the leather-bound books in the oak bookcases surrounding the fireplace. We three children cuddled together on the sofa in our pajamas before bedtime, and I remember she read to us from O. Henry and others, including the poems of Robert Service. His poem "Carry On" gave me chills when she first read it to us. I kept going back to it when I could read and memorized it in bits and pieces over the years.

Mom was also passionate about us learning to read as soon as possible. She bought us the Dick and Jane readers before we started school. They were the "secular version" I figured out later, because at St. Joseph's School, Dick and Jane went to church, and there were crucifixes in their homes (the "Cathedral Editions"). It was a good strategy—she created three avid readers—except for the fact we were bored in class because we knew how most of the stories turned out.

When we were pre-teens, reading stacks of library books on our own, she bought us a long-playing album featuring "The Legend of Sleepy Hollow" on one side and "The Tell-Tale Heart" on the other. We all sat in the living room, a rare event, listening together on the stereo console bought when money was abundant. I was frightened every time, especially at the end, during the increasingly loud, beating sound of the hideous heart when Poe's narrator is being interrogated by the police.

We did not lose everything overnight. Many families of that era experienced robust incomes and comfortable lifestyles, but my Dad had even more income than most, and he seemed to spend it freely on material goods. Our family life at home was already breaking apart, despite the luxury goods, his high income, and his law career.

I remember Mom pushing me out the front door in my pajamas, barefoot, into the snow one dark evening before bedtime. She yelled that I should chase Dad to his car and beg him not to leave. He refused to stop and I felt terrible. Mom got all of us children in the second car and followed him to the High Bridge, where he got out of his car and walked to the edge, 150 feet above the Mississippi. Mom screamed and we all cried at him not to jump, until he came away from the railing. This happened more than once.

I was sad that Mom seemed to give up after the divorce. Her lovely life was gone, yet even then Dad did not leave her in peace. At some time when I was a teenager, I decided that I would never be financially dependent on a man. That kept me going through law school when I hated it and wanted to drop out.

After Dad left, and after being on welfare for about five years, we were living in survival mode and were angry about it. My brothers and I were teenagers now, all in high school, trying to hide the fact that we were poor, that we lived where things were missing or broken. I took my anger out on Mom sometimes when I could not pretend anymore that things were fine. The car we had briefly was a junker, and it was at the mechanic's shop and she could not pay the bill to get it back. She had promised us a short trip to a lake cabin and had to cancel it. I said something mean when she told me we couldn't go. "I did my utmost," she said.

"Well, your *utmost* wasn't good enough!" I did not like hurting her, but sometimes I hated hurting more.

Somewhere around that time, when we were all angry and hopeless, I saw she had taped up a sheet of lined paper from one of our school notebooks. It hung in the small hallway inside the back door, next to the kitchen. It was her paraphrase of a quote from Milton's *Paradise Lost*, in her unique calligraphy-style writing, and her own wording:

The mind is a place in itself
It can make a Hell of Heaven
or a Heaven of Hell.

No one had ever told me that we could use our minds to make a situation better. I believed and assumed happiness came from outside circumstances. I thought we were all at the mercy of our circumstances: Dad drank, Dad left, Mom got MS, our lives went to hell. With this quotation, she flipped things upside-down.

I think we talked about it. At first I wondered if Mom was just trying to get out of taking responsibility for making things better. Yet I felt excited to think those words might be true. I secretly tried to practice with my own thoughts. It wasn't easy, but I know a few times it worked when nothing else did. That piece of paper hung there for years, greasy and tattered and re-taped. But it stayed up.

Little did I know this belief would be the bedrock of the AA program I found when I was twenty-seven, and at the core of the teachings of the Buddha I discovered after I got cancer the first time. It resonated too when I read Viktor Frankl's *Man's Search for Meaning* and realized what a great gift Mom had given us.

It was hard for me to reconcile the mother who sat in a chair watching daytime television nonstop with the mother who gave us Milton to help us cope. When I tried to read to her after she got sick, I had a motive: I wanted to change her back to what she used to be. I learned decades later that the disease probably altered her mental capacity, and not just her physical abilities, and she had no control over it.

I attempted to read to her from Ernest Becker's *Denial of Death* (so she wouldn't fear her mortality), Kahlil Gibran's *The Prophet* (in particular, the poem about releasing your children like arrows, which I thought might convince her to let me stay out later in high school), and *Between Parent and Teenager*, one of the earliest self-help books for parents. That last one was given to me by the mother of the children I babysat: She told me to give it to my mother. She was being discreet—she knew we had troubles. When I handed it to Mom, she immediately tossed it aside (maybe even threw it across the room). I picked it up and read it myself. It helped me enormously because I had no one else to talk to about my teenager questions. After that, I gave up. She preferred her television talk shows, watching pretty people make chicken recipes.

Mom also tossed aside my encouragement to get help, like when I suggested she go to an MS support group called Main Sail. I thought I could entice her because it was supported by a Minnesota Twins baseball player she liked, Frank Quilici. His sister also had MS. I showed her the glossy pamphlet and gave her my most encouraging soft sell. She said, without pausing, "Why in hell would I want to hear other people's sad stories when I have enough of my own?" That's when I truly gave up on trying to change or engage Mom. Life went on in the same way.

A few days before her death, Mick and I were at her side, sitting on the wide arms of the mechanical vinyl recliner chair she had lived in for almost four months. Mick was patting her hand, and I was offering her 7 Up with a straw. She rarely spoke now.

Suddenly, in a voice that was barely audible, pausing for breath after every few words, she spoke. "Your life—is a book," she said. "The beginning and end—are already written. It is—up to you—to write the middle."

Those were her last words. They did not sound like words from the mother I knew these past years. They seemed to come from somewhere else. Somewhere deep and wise.

IV

ELEVATION

In 1994, JUST BEFORE TURNING forty, I was appointed to the Hennepin County Family Court bench. I took a few weeks off between leaving Legal Aid and starting on the court. Clair and I wanted a special vacation before I started working and while we had no children.

My first choice was not surprising—France. I hoped to revisit Paris and then go to the Brittany coast, where I could take Clair to Normandy for the unforgettable experience of seeing the nearly ten thousand alabaster crosses of the US soldiers who died there, some known and many unknown—as their crosses say, "Known only to God." I wanted him to see the broken concrete on the beach from the temporary harbor the US built and some of the bunkers the German soldiers used. Clair was a military history buff, and he joined the Marines after high school, during the Vietnam War, as a way to get out of his small town in northern Minnesota and to get an education on the GI bill. In fact, because of his Marine background, he convinced me we had to have a bulldog for our first marital pet—the Marine mascot. They are expensive and high maintenance. We found a female in the want ads who was the runt of a show litter: She had an unacceptably small head. We loved her. Sarah was the size of a large pug, but with perfect bulldog coloring and features. In 1994, before bulldogs were popular, she turned a lot of heads when we walked her.

Clair wanted a trip to the Caribbean. I had no interest in

that; I wanted France. Then he pointed out the French island of Martinique. I was intrigued. We found a resort on the beach and booked it. We learned through this trip how to compromise our two very different personalities and tastes, and it was a success. Everyone at the resort except one other couple was from France. I spoke French nonstop, and taught Clair how to order a Co-ca-Cola in French. ("Un Coca, s'il vous plaît.") We enjoyed the local people and their food and I bought a set of spices to bring home. Being immersed in colors, smells, tastes, and sounds so different from our life in Minneapolis was a joy.

Not long after we returned, the family court held a ceremony for me with the judicial officers and family court employees. I invited Clair, of course, as well as my best friend and AA sponsor, Audrey, and her husband, Ken. The judges assembled on a platform in three curved rows facing the audience, all wearing their black robes. The chief judge of Family Court stood at the podium and read a summary of my professional accomplishments. He welcomed me to a round of applause. My fears of speaking publicly rose up as I walked to the podium.

I gave a short acceptance speech, which I had memorized, then tried to make it sound like I was speaking impromptu. It went fine. Next, what we were all there for: the swearing-in. I raised my right hand and swore on a Bible to "uphold all laws and faithfully perform all the duties which I now assume to the best of my ability. So help me God." Clair was invited to come up and "robe me," a long-standing tradition in which a loved one helps you into your black robe for the first time. Weeks before the ceremony, I was measured and fitted for this custom-made robe, with my oversized initials embroidered elegantly inside the back. I zipped it up to more applause and went on to the reception of cake and coffee.

Everyone surrounded me with their congratulations. The official court photographer appeared to shoot various staged photos, then continued taking casual photos, which appeared later in the monthly court newsletter, "Full Court Press." I was overwhelmed by the attention, and my face hurt from smiling. For years afterward my friends referred to this ceremony as my "coronation," which embarrassed me. If I had had my way, I would have slipped in quietly and just started working on a Monday, as I did in every other job.

It always rankled me to read an announcement that "Attorney Jane Doe was recently *elevated* to the Court." Having judges physically sit up higher than others, at a massive marble and mahogany bench, flanked by the American and state flags with ornate eagle finials on top, seemed to say that they know more than you, are better than, higher than, wiser than you. Looking down on people felt all wrong to me, and it was my passion to change this model. I knew the set-up well as a practicing attorney, but not until I personally sat up there did I know in my heart it had to change. It was uncomfortable and often dehumanizing. Although it looked like I was the main character onstage, the judge is actually the audience. The people that appear before judges have the important speaking parts, and judges ought to listen to *them*.

Soon after I was sworn in, I saw more evidence of this false authority everywhere. The law is filled with the noble principles of justice, fairness, and equality, yet the rules and bureaucracy seemed detached from them. The principles I valued and practiced in my daily life such as nurturing and compassion, kindness, creativity, and peacemaking were ridiculed as "too nice." In AA we are taught that "the spiritual life is not a theory—we must live it." I believed that the people working in the court institutions should embody the principles that the legal system is built on.

Instead, the people we were there to serve, many in crisis or with special needs, could be greeted by a crabby or strict bureaucrat, forced to wait in long lines, only to be told by a judge that they filled out the forms all wrong and had to start over. The filing fee was hundreds of dollars, unless they were on the federal poverty scale or had a legal aid lawyer or other financial hardship. They had to fill out more forms and wait even longer to get a judge to approve a fee waiver.

Also clearly missing was a plan for empowering people in need, rather than overpowering them. I wondered if I could be at ease in a system that treats people this way. I felt uncomfortable, personally, even to appear as if I had answers because of where I sat and what I wore. The truth was and still is that everyone has the answers for their own lives within themselves. Changing the system into a kind, respectful, and helpful environment is what I wanted to do. It would take time.

Another flaw that I witnessed was how the legal process reduces everyone's problems to a legal problem. The judge sees only what the lawyers or litigants put in their court papers. It is illegal to do outside research on any issue. We must rule from the evidence before us. The judges who appointed me saw only what I put on my résumé: B.A. *magna cum laude*, J.D. *cum laude*, Manager of the Family Law Division of Legal Aid, founder of my own law firm two years out of law school. In the interview I spoke of my courtroom skills and ability to manage a large staff of attorneys and an overflow of challenging family law cases every day. I had practiced the interview for days.

What my résumé did not tell them is this: I grew up in poverty and on welfare when my abusive and alcoholic lawyer-father lost everything and divorced my mother, who was crippled with multiple sclerosis. I did not tell them I was shamed for being a welfare kid whose father abandoned her. I did not tell them I witnessed my father abuse my mother repeatedly, or that my basic needs for food, safety, and cleanliness were not met. I did not tell them I'd been molested by someone my family trusted. I did not tell them I had selective mutism as a child and never spoke in school, which continued until I discovered alcohol. I did not tell them that I also became alcoholic and that I'd been in recovery for thirteen years when I was appointed. As it turned out, those facts that I was ashamed of would become some of the most valuable experiences I brought to the job.

No wonder I felt more comfortable as a lawyer when standing on the floor next to my clients—many of them people without any societal privileges whatsoever, the poorest of the poor—than as a judge sitting high above them.

I slipped away by myself after the cake and photographs to take a break and also to visit my chambers. I sat in the leather desk chair for a long moment looking at the wall of law books and the lone vase of yellow tulips I'd brought and placed on the empty expanse of my new desk. In a few days, families would fill my daily docket and my courtroom expecting me to solve their conflicts and relieve their pain, then write it all up neatly in a court order that they would live by and that we hoped everyone involved would obey. No law book contained what I needed to do this job; I think I already knew that.

Seeing the events from the perspective of those who suffered, while being in a position of privilege and power, was a gift. Many professionals or those with power over others, or those with extra privileges, are unaware of what it is really like to be poor, abused, voiceless, and lost in addiction. Many judges come from Ivy League colleges and law schools and large elite law firms. Some are still compassionate and do understand the problems even though they did not have to live in these circumstances. For me, being granted this unusual place in the world, I realized that what used to be a shameful and painful history could now be an asset. I already had what I needed to do this job.

I got up and walked through my empty courtroom and knew I had to start right there, in that room, and stop saying to myself that I had to eradicate the broken parts of me to do a good job—because suddenly they were important. I could also stop worrying about how to change the entire court system. I knew from AA that its members consider it a "program of attraction, not promotion," which grew from just two men into an international organization. If what I was about to do was right, others would join me willingly.

In addition to navigating the legal process, the people who

used the courts were also dealing with personal crises. Separation from spouse and children, lack of home or money, victims of abuse. I wanted to make it easier for people to have direct and immediate access to me, bypassing the dizzying maze of rules. I wanted them to see me as a fellow human being, not some authority figure. During childhood and adulthood, my family and I were heartlessly pounded down by institutional systems: educational, religious, medical, legal, and governmental. I planned to do it differently.

After I hung my robe in the closet and turned off the lights in my chamber, I took one last look back at the empty space. I would have many families in here when I returned on Monday. I hoped this could be my chance to lift them up.

DAY ONE

I WALKED INTO CHAMBERS ONE hour before court started Monday to a foot-high stack of files in the center of my desk, some fat and some thin, with the printed docket on top—name of case, name of lawyers if any, time of hearing, type of case. Every twenty minutes, another case was scheduled to begin.

I went out into the courtroom, where my clerk's desk was installed next to the bench. I needed to check the accuracy of this schedule. I'd inherited Janet, a thirty-year veteran, with the courtroom. I didn't know her, and I'd heard mixed reviews from the others about her.

"Um, Janet, is this right?" I showed her the docket sheet. "Is it true we schedule cases every twenty minutes no matter what they are? Simple or contested?"

"Yes, Your Honor," Janet said. She explained that is what Admin and the bench had ordered. She told me there was a quota of divorces that must close quickly each year to meet national standards. Plus, the number of cases coming in was increasing.

"You might find we go through lunch hour a lot," Janet said. "Many do cancel at the last minute, so we overbook. If one cancels, you can spend more time on another case. When they all show up, it is crazy. I bring a sandwich every day and eat at my desk behind my computer while you are up there listening to attorneys go on and on. Unfortunately, *you* can't eat up there."

She then told me about a judge who did eat on the bench,

bringing her tray of food from the cafeteria and eating it in front of the litigants. Janet kept calling me "Your Honor," and I asked her to call me Sue, but she was a traditional clerk and never did in all the years she worked with me.

I hurried back to my chambers to read the morning files. First up were two "temporary hearings," a type of proceeding I found to be hellish and highly adversarial when I'd practiced as a family lawyer. The parties were newly separated and couldn't agree on anything. Generally, one spouse did not see the divorce coming and was wounded, rageful, or both. Many of those hurting spouses hired "sharks" for attorneys—cut-throat warriors who feared nothing and put all the dirty laundry into the court papers even though the rules forbid such tactics.

Next, a simple and amicable divorce with full agreements, then two motions to increase child support, another simple hearing, then a complicated motion to stop alimony due to unemployment. That was just the morning.

I could feel the signs of my former social phobia rising: pounding heart, shaky hands, dry mouth. One friendly colleague ran by in her robe before starting her calendar and poked her head in. "Good luck Susie Q!" she said. "If you are like us, this job will be like a trauma ER for the first few weeks. It gets better."

Another one stopped by to wish me well. She said, "A word to the wise: After the deputy says *All rise*, don't forget to say *Please be seated*. On my first day, I was moving right along in my first case when my clerk crept up behind me and handed me a note: 'They are still standing. Tell them they can sit down.'"

I went back to reading my files, smiling at that image. Their brief supportive welcome visits helped. I was still reading when Janet stepped in and said, "Showtime, your Honor!"

I went to the closet, hung up my suit jacket, and zipped the new robe over my clothes, checked my make-up, put on some lipstick, combed my hair, and picked up all the files. I clutched them tightly as I walked to the courtroom door. In less than a month I would call this process *putting on my armor.*

As I imagined sitting up high on the bench in a few moments, I felt real fear. I paused to take some deep breaths before I opened the courtroom door to go in.

I quickly went up the stairs behind the bench and sat down just before the first people came in—so the deputy would not have to say "All rise" when I walked in. All I could do was keep breathing and trust the words I needed would come out. I planned to be a kind and fair judge who treated all people with dignity. That day had arrived.

Two women sat on one side of the large table and two men at the other. One marriage, two lawyers. The lawyers sat in front of their clients, Mr. and Mrs. Johnson. At this type of hearing, a motion, the clients did not testify or even say a word. All of their information and statements were typed up and signed under oath in sworn affidavits. Those were filed weeks ago, and I'd just read them. The lawyers would make oral arguments now, and it was my job to make sure they did not stray outside what they wrote and filed weeks ago.

This couple had been married a dozen years, and at first she was a homemaker and took care of their two children during the day. The children were now in school, aged eight and ten, a boy and a girl, and the mother worked in the school. The husband was in sales, and his income fluctuated in the past five years between sixty and eighty thousand dollars. One year it spiked to over one hundred thousand, but he claimed that was a one-time contract and would never happen again. Her lawyer used this amount as his base income, which was deceptive. They lived in a modest home in a suburb of Minneapolis.

"Good morning," I said. "I will be hearing your case today and will issue your order promptly." I was met with silence.

"All right then," I said. "We have twenty minutes for your case to be argued. Counsel, you each have ten minutes. Let's begin."

I looked at the wife's attorney because they'd filed for divorce first. Immediately she stood and said, "That's ridiculous. No one else in family court holds us to that time frame."

I was shocked at how she spoke to me. Inside I cringed. I could not imagine messing up my very first case. I could halt the hearing and run down the hall and ask someone if what she said was true, but they were probably all in court now, too. I decided on the spot to stick with it because of what my clerk said, and also so the rest of the people did not have to wait excessively for their twenty-minute hearings.

"All of your information has been filed," I replied. "You cannot bring in new evidence, so just highlight whatever you feel is important during your oral argument. I read everything beforehand." She shook her head, sat down, and muttered something under her breath, like "This is crazy." Her client looked stricken and whispered to her lawyer. I said directly to her, "Ms. Johnson. No need to worry. The law requires every fact to be filed in here—I held up the file—two weeks before the court date. To avoid unfair surprise, the rule says that neither one of you can raise brand new issues today. I have read everything carefully and will listen closely to the arguments before writing my order. Let's begin." Five minutes had already ticked away.

The wife's attorney stood up holding the affidavit she'd filed, a long rambling statement the wife signed under oath about her budget, her children, and her need to stay in the house and get alimony (spousal maintenance). The attorney was reading it line-by-line, which was completely unnecessary after I said I read it. I wondered if she was being oppositional or just was not a very good lawyer. I let it go, being my first case and all, and at exactly ten minutes I interrupted her and said, "Thank you counsel. Your time is up."

She looked angry. "I am going to talk to the Chief Judge about this," she said. "It's a travesty to put in all this work and only get ten minutes."

I realized then I was cutting into her billable hours.

"Remember," I said, "these hearings are based on your written material, you cannot add new evidence, and you had your time for argument. You chose to read the document *verbatim* to

me, although I said I already read it. Let's move on now." I immediately felt my stomach constricting for reacting with annoyance
and a touch of anger.

Her face was bright red as she wrote furiously on a legal pad.
This is not how I'd planned to be on the bench. Rigid and stern.
I'd imagined I would be a kind, generous listener, a peaceful re-
solver of disputes. If I were totally honest, I would have admitted
I thought I would be Christ-like. Accepting, forgiving, gentle, and
wise.

Later that day I asked around and found out most judges just
let the attorneys run the hearing without time limits, while the
other people (usually those without attorneys) had to wait outside
the courtroom for hours sometimes. It was in actuality a "mass
calendar"—reserved appointments were meaningless. Temporary hearings would take the most time of everything except a
trial. You had to decide every single issue without any live testimony. There is a lot riding on that ruling: who gets temporary
residency of the house, how often a parent can be with their children, how much of the income goes to each party.

The next attorney, looking fresh out of law school, took the
opposite tack. "Your Honor, I will be very brief here," he said.
"Two minutes." He made a grandiose gesture to look at his
watch. "You will see in the tax returns my client attached to his
affidavit that he makes nowhere near what she claims. She is asking for outrageous sums of money, full custody, no time for the
father to be with the children—clearly, she is being punitive. Yes,
he has a girlfriend, and yes, his wife is hurting, but unfortunately
that happens, and the law says she cannot take away the children
without proof of endangerment. As his affidavit shows, he has
been an active, loving father who provided for his family. Their
children will be the innocent victims if they can't see their father.
This family lived frugally to save for their children's college and
their retirement. Used cars, no luxury vacations, small house. He
worked from home quite a bit and was there for his children daily.

We know you are learned in the laws and you will make the correct decisions. That is all. Thank you."

He looked at his watch again and smiled and nodded at me and sat down. The other attorney jumped up. "I need rebuttal time! He is spending lavishly on his girlfriend and dissipating marital assets!"

"You covered all that by attaching his credit card statements showing the restaurants, hotels, jewelry, and women's clothing purchases," I said. "We are out of time. I will make the decision from here."

She looked at me with tight lips. She stood quickly and began packing her briefcase.

I said, "I have a request of the parties. Mr. and Ms. Johnson, would you be willing to meet with our court mediator? They are right across the hall. There is no charge."

Their stony faces never budged. I assumed the attorneys had advised them not to mediate because that would reduce their fees. I told them that studies showed how hard a contested divorce is on the children (I knew from actual experience as a child but never mentioned that publicly) and some of my other favorite facts designed to alert parents to the horrors and costs of the court and to convince them to try mediation. "Did you know that 95 percent of all cases settle before trial?" I asked. "Why not settle now and save your money for your children? Why not keep control of your family and make these important decisions about your children's and your futures yourselves, in private, instead of turning it over to me, a total stranger?"

The wife's attorney interrupted before I could finish. "Can we go now?"

Again her rudeness shocked me. Quickly I responded, "Yes." I wanted this over. I got up while the attorneys were still packing up their briefcases and went down the stairs to get to my chambers.

I'd gone over by ten minutes. I had to get right back out there for another hearing, almost identical to the previous one. Children, an affair, not enough money for two households, rage. Janet came back to my chambers and said, "Well, you started your judicial career off with one of the nastiest pit bulls. Good to see you put a heavy leash on her. Bravo!"

I told her I was just trying to keep to the schedule so people didn't have to wait hours for their twenty-minute hearing, which took them six weeks to get. "This case was not that complicated and it was all in the file," I said. "Anyway, I thought all the judges stuck to the calendar."

I didn't like being so stern in there, but I saw no workable alternative. Would my name now be mud in the bar association? I wondered if the lawyer would complain to the Chief Judge. Little did I know that the behavior management of attorneys would be just one of my many daunting tasks.

"Some good news," Janet said. "The second temporary hearing settled the whole divorce. They called in and canceled while you were on the first one. I could have run a note up to you but I liked the way you told her what was what. I was afraid if you knew you had more time you might give in to her!"

I had made an enemy of the lawyer and a friend of my clerk. I went into chambers, made a cup of tea, and used the extra few minutes to read files. Janet came in and took the other temporary hearing file away and said, "This will be coming in as a full written settlement in one week. I will hound them if we do not receive it by then."

I smiled. "Great. My first settled case and I did absolutely nothing."

"Maybe they got wind of the new sheriff in town!" She laughed and walked out.

Janet quickly became an integral part of this operation, handling hundreds of details, answering every phone call, opening every courier delivery and piece of mail, which allowed me to do only my courtroom work and then write my orders. She never compared me to the previous judges she had clerked for. I got through the morning without any further drama, and at 12:30 p.m. I was done. I felt exhausted.

"Take a nice long lunch, walk or go shopping," Janet said. "The whole afternoon fell apart."

"What does *that* mean? 'It fell apart . . .'"

"It means everyone called in and cancelled. Either they settled, both sides agreed to continue it for some reason, or they did not get their papers served on the other side."

"What a waste of the court calendar! Do attorneys run this calendar by calling you directly?"

"Yes."

"And you have to give them what they want? And there are no consequences when they cancel the same day?"

"That is all correct."

"Think of all the others waiting six weeks to get in here. Doctors and dentists would not stand for that. Why do *we*?"

She shrugged and I filed that away and frankly was glad to have the afternoon to work on that morning order for the Johnson family. I took a brisk walk over the Mississippi River on the Stone Arch Bridge. Halfway across I leaned on the cool concrete edge, watching the flow of the river below me.

I thought again about the first hearing. I agreed with the "pit bull" lawyer. It was wrong to restrict the sides to ten minutes each. This hearing represented the clients' lives. They were in crisis. They deserved more.

I knew that calendars needed to be run by the court and not by the whim of the attorneys. I would schedule longer hearings. More time for complicated matters. Shorter times for simple defaults. Tailor them to the type of case, just as I did as a lawyer in my client meetings. Common sense. No wonder people disliked the court. The intimidating appearance, a labyrinth to get to the judge, and then less than a half hour with her?

We needed an all-new case management system. In truth, we had *no* case management system. The original system started when times were different, not when fifty per cent of all marriages ended in divorce. When my parents divorced, we were the only family in the Catholic school for years who had divorced parents and the only one in the neighborhood. I used to lie and tell the neighbor kids Dad was out of town after he moved out. On school forms, I wrote "deceased."

I knew I also needed to stop those vicious temporary hearings altogether. They created more mistrust, hatred, and greed between the parents as soon as a case was filed. Once the accusatory words were typed and handed to the spouse, just seeing them printed in a legal document had a powerful and damaging effect. Not to mention these are all public documents for anyone to read, including the children when they are older. The parents could not look at each other afterward, much less collaborate.

I saw one tiny opening where I could start: the very first contact that people have with the court. I would talk to my two new judicial friends about my ideas and get their opinion on how I could go about changing the scheduling process. I found out there was indeed a hierarchical web —one that resisted change. This large system that needed major changes left me feeling small and powerless. As the years went on, I continued to take that walk across the river when I could, as a way to clear my head and to think things through.

In 1994, the same year I was appointed, a Buddhist nun named Pema Chodrön published a book called *Start Where You Are: A Guide to Compassionate Living.* I discovered it soon afterward and found in it principles that gave me strength to persevere in my quest to reform the courts. She encouraged us to "start where we are" by embracing rather than denying the painful parts of our lives. I saw the possibility that one imperfect person could change an institution, and, later, how she could face even cancer with courage and equanimity.

MISDIAGNOSIS

In 1999, when I was forty-four years old, I found a lump on the outside of my left breast while taking a bath. I had just tucked all three boys in bed. My ritual after working in the courtroom all day, then making dinner and heading to the playground with my husband and the three boys, was to get them to bed, then sink into a steamy bath with eucalyptus bath oil.

When I felt the lump, my body froze. I hugged my knees, teeth chattering. I told Clair about it when I got into bed and he looked terrified. Then he said, "I am sure it will be benign." He was not one for talking about feelings, so I wanted to do that with my sponsor and friend Audrey as soon as possible. We had an inside joke: "It hasn't happened until we have talked about it." The next morning I told Audrey, and she agreed I should make an urgent appointment with my primary care physician. While the doctor silently examined the lump, I started shaking. I clasped my hands over my abdomen to try to stop.

"You're not *scared*, are you?" she asked. I remember her tone. It was mocking, teasing.

I *was* terrified. I said, "It's just that I never get lumps or bumps or cysts like my friends do. Yes. I am concerned."

"Sorry," she said. "I was trying to put you at ease. I'm sure it's nothing. Eighty percent of lumps are benign."

Audrey told me her doctor aspirated her lumps right in the office. If it was just fluid, it was nothing to worry about. This doctor, from the same clinic, didn't offer to do that. I didn't ask for it. "If you are still worried, I can refer you to an expert surgeon," she said. A look of horror must have crossed my face. "Relax," she added. "This is just to ease your mind. And if there is cancer, which is highly unlikely given your age, you will want to know about her. She is the best."

I immediately scheduled the first available appointment with the surgeon. It was a week away. I had to move a trial, which was very difficult for me to do. People waited weeks or months for their trial date and had everything prepared. I had never changed a trial date before for personal reasons, but this time I did. I don't remember if I asked Clair to go with me, or, if I did, why he was unable to go. When I showed up at the surgeon's office, the shaking started again. I checked in and the receptionist said, "Ma'am, your appointment is not until tomorrow."

How frightened I must have been to arrive a day early! In all my years practicing law I was never late for court. And certainly never a day early.

Back again the next day, I sat stiffly in the lobby. After what seemed like an hour, I was led into an examination room and put on a gown. The doctor was a large woman with long blonde hair and big glasses. She wore a loose shift dress with an oversized floral print. No lab coat. With her was a medical school intern. The doctor asked if I minded if the intern observed. I shook my head. She began chatting about just returning from Hawaii. Maybe she's trying to put me at ease, I thought, but I wanted to be taken seriously. Here was a renowned surgeon and she thought I cared that she went to Hawaii and had fun while I'm going through this? The medical student stood quietly in the corner.

The student watched as the surgeon felt the lump, pressing with both hands, up, down, side-to-side. It seemed endless. She asked many questions while she did this, like whether I had ever had a lump or cyst before and if my breasts changed during my period at all. The answer was always no.

"I doubt this is breast cancer," she said, "but I will do an ultrasound and then that way we can tell if it's a lump or just a cyst."

She sent me right into their ultrasound room and I was grateful I didn't have to reschedule another afternoon of cases.

After the ultrasound, the technician told me to wait in the lobby until I was called back in to see the surgeon and hear the results. When I saw her again, she said, "Good news," and she showed me the black-and-white image of the inside of my breast. "This ultrasound image shows that the lump is not solid. It's filled with fluid. That means it's a benign cyst." I was relieved, yet skeptical.

"How can you be positive it's not cancer without a biopsy?"

She repeated, with a touch of annoyance in her voice, "I told you. This shows definitively that it is filled with fluid. Cancer is solid and appears entirely differently. If it's *bothering* you I can take it out."

I thought for a moment. No, it didn't *bother* me physically. It didn't hurt. But I did not want a lump in my breast. What woman would? It bothered me emotionally, not physically. She made me feel like I was a nuisance because I did not like this lump in my breast.

"No," I said. "It doesn't hurt." I knew she expected me to say that.

"Good." She explained that most women do have lumps from time to time but "they go away."

I looked at her, with all the courage I had, and said, "I have three boys. The oldest is only four years old. They were adopted as babies and already lost their birth parents. I can't take a risk and have them lose another mother. Are you one hundred percent positive this is not cancer? Would you put that in writing?" This sounds bizarre to me now, but I thought that if she was wrong and I died, at least my family could sue her for wrongful death or medical malpractice.

"Of course," she said. "I'll send you a letter." She walked out. I got dressed. I was still unsettled.

Even with my intelligence, my law degree, my strong advocacy skills for my clients, my appointment to the judiciary and a position of authority, I could not stand up to her and demand a biopsy or removal of the lump. Nor did I get another opinion. I had three young boys, a busy career, and I had already missed work three times for this lump. Why would I keep investigating it when she was so positive and the ultrasound said it could not possibly be cancer?

She gave me an answer I should have been happy to receive, but it was not satisfying or reassuring. I now know that my body was trying to tell me something. I heard and felt the message, to keep going, but I did not listen.

I crossed my arms at work and my hidden right hand checked countless times through my blouses to see if it was still there, every day. It was.

My last check point was my best friend, Audrey. "How can this doctor know it's not cancer without a biopsy?" I asked her.

"She has seen inside women's breasts," Audrey told me. "She knows what cancer feels like." She added, "There was the ultrasound. You saw this all the way through."

By now Audrey had been my AA sponsor for seventeen years and was still my best friend. She was older, and, in my opinion, wiser than me. I admired her from the day I met her, I think, because she was sober for so long and I had just crawled in the door, my life a mess. Even though I now had all these years of sobriety, I felt she knew better than me, and I trusted her advice. She had taught me the AA program and helped save my life. I could not contradict her. Had she told me to get a biopsy I would have.

The surgeon wrote her letter, which said, as I requested, *"Susan Cochrane has a simple fluid-filled cyst in her left breast. She should return in a year for her routine mammogram."*

I did not get my annual mammogram. I waited almost two years and this time I was instructed to get a biopsy immediately. I went in for the biopsy. Same lump. Afterward, I could not warm up, even under the warm blankets they gave me. As I rested, two doctors came in. One stood on each side of my bed and their faces told me everything.

They said they would call me with the results. I talked to them about my life, my three beautiful boys, my career. The early intervention court program I designed. My recent trip to Russia to train judges and police on how we handle domestic abuse cases in the United States. They listened carefully to everything. They weren't acting like doctors; they were acting like people who cared about me. People who knew I had advanced cancer and were being kind.

After two days of no one calling, I called them back. A nurse told me over the telephone I had cancer and would need to see a surgeon right away. Shockwaves pulsed through my body.

I told Clair and Audrey, who rushed over to my house and cried with me, but I did not tell anyone at work. I did not know what this meant to my life yet. The next morning I was scheduled to speak to a group of parents in the courthouse auditorium, people who had just filed for divorce, as part of the divorce education program we provided. I was in shock, but I made it through. I could see myself from a distance giving the speech. I remember saying, "Yes, divorce is painful. You will recover, but it takes time. There are many families, maybe even yourselves, who have experienced tragedies like cancer, death of a loved one, financial problems. There are many serious challenges in life. How you react to these challenges is what is most important. If you face it head on, allow the pain to be present, deal with the grief and pain responsibly, you will get through this. And you will still have the respect and love of your children and a decent life afterward. You will model to them how to face a crisis with courage. Some are not so lucky." I was picturing my mother's despair. I think I also was giving myself a pep talk on how to face this cancer diagnosis.

I went back to the medical center that did the biopsy to discuss the diagnosis, and a different surgeon said, "Good thing we caught it early!"

I finally lost my temper. "That is a lie! Your top breast surgeon said it was a simple cyst. We could have gotten it out the first time

I brought it in two years ago." I told him I wanted all my files and I was switching hospitals immediately.

I sat in the lobby of the new breast surgeon the very next morning. They rushed me into their schedule at 9:00 a.m. This center was known for patient-centered care and had its own breast center. I was already impressed and getting inspiration for how the courts could better welcome the litigants.

While I sipped hot tea from a china cup and saucer, Clair was across town, waiting for my films and files at the other medical center's front desk. The young receptionist, unaware of my story, let it slip that a team of surgeons and doctors were reviewing my films and files before they released them to us. I suspected their lawyer was in there too. I called Clair and said, "Demand my records immediately, then get in the car and race them over to me. I'm about to see the surgeon who is going to do the mastectomy and she needs them right now. Tell them if they refuse, I'll file a lawsuit for malpractice, negligence, and interference with my medical care!" I made up that last claim. He answered "Okay" rather meekly and hung up.

Despite being a prosecutor, a body-builder, and a Marine veteran, Clair is conflict-avoidant, as some call it. But this time he must have said something like I suggested, because they handed everything over. Giant manila envelopes of x-ray films, smaller ones with documents and discs. He got them to me just in time, while we were still in the exam room. The surgeon told us both it was a very "grave situation" and sent me directly to an MRI. As soon as she saw the results of the MRI, she recommended a double mastectomy, which would have removed my healthy breast as well, but I opted not to have both breasts removed at once—I could not handle that right now.

She told me the tumor was one-tenth of a centimeter from my chest wall and spreading. She thought it was in my lymph nodes as well, and we could find that out during surgery. Despite it being Thanksgiving week, we scheduled the surgery.

There was another wrenching aspect of that experience,

which I did not want to tell anyone about. I knew it was my fault the cancer was so far advanced. I had not insisted on a biopsy or a second opinion, or returned for another mammogram in a year.

I was overcome with terror about dying and leaving my three young boys. I could not imagine dying with my oldest just starting first grade and the twins in kindergarten. My mother had died when I was twenty-four, and the pain was unbearable. Now, my rage at the surgeon who'd misdiagnosed the lump and at myself was constant. One day a nurse referred me to Nancy, a "healing counselor," someone who supposedly would listen and guide me through my strong emotions. Nancy was a former nurse, kind and smart. She encouraged me to talk about whatever I wanted. I spent the first few sessions sobbing about my mother's death. When I apologized for that, she said I could trust myself and just allow all my thoughts and feelings to come up without analyzing them.

At one point in our sessions, I told her about my gross negligence in not following up on the lump. I wondered if I had an unconscious death wish, because I'd known deep inside that the lump was cancer no matter what the surgeon said. I'd felt it every day and worried, but I'd pushed my worry aside. I also thought that my history of mutism and shyness contributed to me being intimidated by that surgeon and not speaking up. I hated myself for that, too.

Nancy helped me see that other women could reasonably have believed and accepted the surgeon's diagnosis. The scan definitively showed it was not cancer and also, at my age, it was unlikely that I had cancer. Since it was "a simple cyst," it made sense to rely on the expert's opinion and to delay getting a mammogram.

After several months of weekly meetings with Nancy, I could talk about the misdiagnosis without rage or tears. I still was sad about the choices I made. I could perhaps have caught it in stage one had I demanded the lump be removed or just biopsied. At least I learned experts and diagnostic machines are not infallible, and I would always get a second opinion on important medical matters in the future.

After the mastectomy, my new doctor referred me to a plastic surgeon for the reconstruction. He would be an integral part of my recovery for many months thereafter. He was one of the kindest doctors I have ever met, gentle and understanding. During the examination, he assured me that the left breast would not show any scars and would be perfectly shaped, as well as "lifted." Then he looked at my right breast (which I chose not to have proactively removed), and he said I could absolutely keep the "elegant drape of the mature breast," if I so desired. I smiled for the first time in weeks. I loved him and his choice of words in that moment. He added that insurance would pay for a mastopexy (breast lift) so it would match the reconstructed breast, if I wished to have that outcome. I chose the matching, non-draping set.

The evening before the surgery, I couldn't sleep. I lay on the living room floor, listening to the same CD over and over through my earphones. It was one of those compilations of popular songs from the past year I'd impulsively bought at the drugstore counter earlier that day. I listened to songs of love and loss while tears dripped from the sides of my eyes and into my ears. I slid my right hand under my pajama top and caressed my left breast. It felt warm, soft, and perfectly shaped. This was my good-bye. In eight hours, everything but the skin would be gone.

At 7:00 a.m., Audrey took me to the plastic surgeon's office while Clair got the three boys fed, dressed, and ready for school. The surgeon carefully measured and marked both breasts multiple times with a permanent black marker. When finished, he asked if I would allow a "before" picture that would not show my face. I gladly agreed, because when I saw his portfolio of before-and-after photographs of other women's surgeries, it helped me get through my fear of looking ugly or mutilated afterward.

My left breast tissue was completely removed through the circle of the areola, as well as all lymph nodes under my left arm. The skin of my entire armpit and surrounding areas would be permanently numb but the surgeon said the brain compensates by helping us "forget about it."

A small piece of skin from my back became my new areola. A year later the plastic surgeon would artfully create a nipple, then tattoo the area a natural pink color. I was amazed when I looked in the mirror. It clearly was reconstructed, but looked better than I thought it would.

After the mastectomy, the pathology report said that the lymph nodes under my left arm were "grossly replaced by tumors." I went home with four tubes draining blood from my chest and back into soft plastic bulbs, which I emptied every few hours. I had a latissimus flap reconstruction, not as popular as most procedures, but it allowed me to be all done in one day rather than return weekly for adjustments. Even with strong pain medication, I hurt all over. I found comfort reading the twins to sleep, then scrunching into one of their tiny beds, blue beds with teddy bear headboards. I cried silently while I held onto one of them while they slept, every night for weeks.

Mastectomy, chemotherapy, radiation. A year off work. I had ten cancer-free years after that.

The first few years after surgery, I lived with the realistic fear that the cancer would soon return and I would die. Triple negative breast cancer is well-known to recur quickly within two to five years. There is no ongoing treatment as there is for other breast cancers. I went to counseling to discuss how to handle my death with three young adopted boys, and it helped, but I still felt terrified of that result. Two years after the treatments, my oncologist found a mass on one of my ovaries after a CAT scan, a common spot for triple negative cancer to recur. I prepared for the worst with my counselor, but Clair was not open to talking about my death. He kept saying, "It is not going to be cancer."

We were all shocked to find out the tumor was a rare sort of benign tumor, and we were ecstatic. It was then, after that scare, in 2005, that I decided to go to the Commonweal retreat center. It is in a remote section of the Pacific Coast and is designed for cancer patients at all stages of their journeys. The retreat price was intentionally affordable, but we still needed to borrow some money from retirement in order to get me there for a whole week. There were many outstanding medical bills, not to mention my unpaid leave from work for that year, a major setback financially.

The Commonweal retreat was a powerful experience in my life. I shared my fears of dying in our group of eight, received caring help from our facilitator, learned to meditate, did yoga each morning, ate organic foods, climbed down the rocky shore to the crashing waves, received massages, and made friends.

While there, I participated in a session of sand-tray therapy, a Jungian hands-on healing technique. The process involves selecting a basketful of items from shelves packed with hundreds of clay figures, birds, jewels, and other objects, and then arranging them on a large open table filled with sand. I was intimidated and anxious about choosing the right objects, but the facilitator said to be like a child and let my hand move without thinking. Alone with the facilitator, I had ample time to choose and place my items. Once I was finished, the facilitator offered an interpretation. "You had a mastectomy on the left side," she began. I asked how she could know that. She showed me that out of the dozens of clay figures, I had chosen a small figure of a woman on her knees, her arms raised triumphantly. I had placed her in the center of the tray, in front of an open treasure chest that was overflowing with jewels. I looked closer and saw she was missing her left breast. I still have the photograph of my tray.

In my final interview with co-founder Michael Lerner, I tried to tell him that everything seemed brighter and clearer now. I asked how I could take this feeling and experience home, where there was stress and conflict. He answered, "I just try to stand in the light." The retreat and the people who were there changed me, opened me to the possibilities of a spiritual life beyond the twelve steps of AA. I was excited to bring what I learned home with me. I started by finding a meditation center.

When my bone scan in 2011 came back with evidence of cancer almost everywhere in my skeleton, my oncologist ordered a bone biopsy from my hip. She explained I had stage four cancer. I could tell I had changed from being "me," someone she chatted with as a friend about our children and our work for the past ten years, into a "diagnosis" of terminal cancer. I was in shock and asked a lot of questions, and she kept smiling, and even said, "Don't worry. We will do this dance together."

I had three children, young teens now, had a career, and was going to die from cancer. This was not a dance. I could not stand her at that moment.

I had a court docket filled six months out. I tried to tell her about that. She smiled but ignored me, kept writing on her computer. She sent a team of nurses and techs in their white coats, with their clipboards and calendars, to schedule the surgery, under anesthesia, that would put a chemotherapy port into my chest next day. I would be subjected to two kinds of extremely powerful intravenous chemo at once—just like ten years ago when I got sick as anything, with low white blood cell counts, and then shingles and no energy. And I'd gone bald of course. That was when I was more than ten years younger and did not have stage four. Now I could not imagine I would last long, and I knew I would probably not feel well for whatever was left of my life.

I learned a very hard lesson when I didn't listen to myself when that lump was discovered twelve years before. This time I stood up out of the chair, took Clair's arm, and walked out. I was feeling physically well at that point in time. I was exercising three times a week at a gym and walking every day at lunch. Our kids were doing well. Clair and I had bought a new home on a tiny lake in the center of the city, which I loved. I meditated, took writing and mindfulness classes, and saw my dream of writing becoming real.

I realized that if I did have to go down the path of chemotherapy, sickness, and possibly death, then I wanted to do it near my home at the cancer center that treated me after the misdiagnosis ten years ago. I called my former breast surgeon and she immediately referred me to a research oncologist. When I met with him, his first words were, *We have time.* What a contrast from the battery of nurses trying to schedule surgery to put a chemo port in my chest without regard to my needs, my court docket, and my family. I was still in shock. I was so relieved he said we had time. He wanted to look at non-chemotherapy options.

"There is some brand-new research out there," he explained. "I am going to look into it." I settled down and trusted how he acted slowly and thoughtfully. I have endless gratitude for having listened to my own voice this time, for not staying with the other oncologist, where I would already have had a round of chemo poured in through a port in my chest.

Ten years earlier, they'd asked if I would donate my breast tissue to science. I'd felt stupid and selfish when I'd told them no. Because of that decision, it had been put in storage, and now the oncologist could go back and retest my tissue.

It turned out the cancer was androgen hormone receptor positive. Treatable with an androgen-blocking pill instead of chemo. Manageable side effects. A treatment that was not even on the radar a few years earlier. A treatment my first oncologist had not been aware of.

This made all the difference. My new oncologist discovered a tiny study of twenty-five women—women using androgen blockers, just like the ones men take for prostate cancer—because some breast cancer seeks androgen too.

My oncologist once said he did not treat medical records; he treated the person sitting in front of him.

When I knew him better, I asked him why he didn't just go with the standard chemotherapy when the bone biopsy clearly showed I still had triple negative cancer. I will never forget what he said.

"Sometimes you have to listen to that small voice inside." His small voice gave me my life. I try to listen to mine now, too.

BOYS

GROWING UP, I WAS THE only girl between two brothers, each of us one year apart. I was the classic 1960s tomboy: hair in braids, grimy from head to toe all summer long from playing baseball or building a go-cart in the garage. I broke both arms (not at the same time): the first playing football and the other jumping from a tree. I took breaks from the outdoor action to play piano and guitar, to read, to sew, to create a world of puppets, and to do all manner of arts and crafts. I often dreamed of having a daughter, but if I had boys, I certainly knew a bit about them. When the time came, I chose boys.

Clair and I were in our forties when we decided to adopt a baby. We'd always wanted children, but given our ages, the doctor said after one year of trying to get pregnant, it was time for us to look into either medical intervention or adoption. So we chose to proceed with an international adoption from Korea because Audrey's two children were from there. I imagined our child would be like a cousin to them and, I hoped, would find comfort in sharing their heritage.

The age cut-off for an adoptive parent of a child from Korea was forty-five. Clair was nearly there, and I wasn't far behind. Our law careers were already established, and given our ages, we made the assumption that one child would be enough for us. We both came from families of three children and that was our first preference, but we understood it was impossible given the

Korean regulation, so we became comfortable with the plan for just one child.

After filling out the tall stack of application papers, we learned from our social worker that there was a long waiting list for Korean baby girls and none for Korean baby boys. To get a baby before my husband went over the age limit, we would need to accept a boy. We checked "no preference" knowing we would receive a boy, and we happily did—a healthy and beautiful four-month-old baby boy, Lee.

About six months after he arrived, instead of satisfying my hunger for a family, he opened up a faucet of love at full force, not only for him but for another baby. Clair was now over the age limit for Korean adoptions. As I pushed Lee's stroller around the lake, I felt such love for him, while my heart ached because there could be no more children for us. I knew the age limit but called our social worker anyway.

"Sorry, impossible," she said, as she tried to steer us to other countries like China, which had higher age limits. I told her, "Our son already has parents who aren't Korean, and his sibling won't be related by blood, but at least they could all be Korean. I insist on that."

I pressed on. I called her supervisor. The supervisor immediately said we could qualify for another Korean baby at our age if we accepted one with special needs. Since I'd helped care for my mother with her depression and multiple sclerosis until I was twenty-four, and later for Audrey's two adopted children, who both had serious special needs that were discovered as they developed, I thought I was capable of caring for any problems my child might have. I was still fairly new to the family court bench and I did worry about a catastrophic medical situation interfering with my dream job. Even so, I was sure I would adjust my work schedule if necessary to care for this new baby.

Two months later we received a referral for not one, but two more boys.

They were premature identical twins. One was three pounds

and the other four pounds at birth. A teenaged mother, an emergency C-section: that was all we knew. She'd given them beautiful Korean names: Tae-Ho, which means "great radiance"; and Sun-Ho, which translates roughly as "first light." She took them home when they stabilized. The smaller one had a seizure, pneumonia, and other serious problems, and bleeding on the brain was suspected. An MRI was inconclusive. Serious impairments were not ruled out. Both twins were considered special needs due to their low birth weight, and the smaller one might have even more problems. Their birth mother did not have the resources or family support to care for them and made the difficult decision to find them a home in the United States. She made one request—that the twins "be raised in the arts."

We showed our family doctor the single page of information we had. He recommended we get an updated brain MRI of the smaller baby to understand the extent of his situation, and, most important, to be prepared for it. Our special needs social worker strongly advised us against it. "They might decline you as parents after that request," she said. "It could appear you are looking for a perfect baby rather than accepting him just as he is. I know you are not, that you are just getting ready, but they are sensitive."

"We won't back out no matter what the MRI says; we just want to be prepared," I repeated. She convinced us this request could jeopardize the entire adoption, so we let it go.

Clair and I tried to picture life with three boys in diapers, two careers, and one baby who might have serious problems. We wanted the twins, there was no doubt about that. I carried the referral photograph from Korea in my pocket everywhere I went. It was tattered on the edges and wrinkled in the middle. I made more copies of it at the local photo shop. I studied it. It was all we had. The photo was taken from above, with the twins, who were lying flat on their backs side-by-side, arms touching, in matching soft white pajamas on a white sheet and a white background. It was probably taken at a medical clinic. They both had fluffy, inky black hair which stood straight up. The smaller twin looked sad to me, and he had a bit less hair than his brother. The older twin had, I thought, an amused expression. I was already in love with them.

"We need to get them here," I told Clair. "I don't care what issues they have. If I have to quit the court, I will. I don't care if we go broke or end up on welfare. Look, I was raised on welfare." I was exaggerating, but I was certain I was willing to take on two special needs babies with a toddler already in the family. I did not need to say more because Clair desperately wanted them too. Although he worried a lot about money and our future, he agreed we must bring them to our home, no matter what.

THUMPER

IT TURNED OUT THAT OUR first baby boy, Lee, from the "healthy infant" program, had extreme health and behavioral issues that emerged around age two. For the next ten years we treated his symptoms—impulse control, sensory overload, social difficulties, tantrums—with occupational, speech, and physical therapy, plus counseling and medication. He was evaluated by a number of experts, including an adoption expert. Several specialists warned he would need lifelong residential care, meaning institutionalization. All recommended constant intervention. We continually researched new and better services for Lee. I always held out hope that the next thing we tried would be "it."

Through those years, we looked for answers in parenting books. The titles got progressively more frightening to us: *The Out-of-Sync Child*, *The Active-Alert Child*, *The Challenging Child*, *The Difficult Child*, *The Defiant Child*, *The Explosive Child*.

From age seven though eleven, Lee had weekly therapy with a psychologist. We were not allowed in the sessions, but we could hear them playing board games and talking. We trusted her, and when she recommended we call the police or an ambulance anytime he displayed out-of-control, aggressive behavior, we complied. When upset, he would scream and swear, and throw whatever was near. At home, he damaged electronics, furniture, and the walls. He ran away from school. Once he tried to jump from a moving car.

The experts stressed the need for behavior management and strict consequences, but this did not make a difference. We felt like terrible parents. The school system concluded Lee had oppositional defiant disorder with anxiety, and no one questioned it further. Not even me.

Extreme episodes resulted in Lee being admitted to the children's hospital for inpatient psychiatric services three separate times by the time he was eleven years old. On his third admission to the hospital, the intake worker at the emergency room asked me, "I see he has been here a few times for the same thing. Does his behavior get worse when people try to restrain him?"

"Absolutely, yes."

"Is he unable to remember the consequences from his last episode when he is under stress? Like it is locked away in a file drawer he cannot access?" Another emphatic yes.

"Have you ever had him tested for autism?"

"No," I said. "One school aide suggested he might have signs but never referred us for testing. None of his current therapists or doctors or schools have ever once suggested that."

We told Lee what the hospital social worker said. He didn't say anything, so I continued. I told him that he was smart and talented but if he had a form of autism, having a diagnosis would help him get into programs that would be more helpful. I explained I found the place where they give a test and he could keep listening to his iPod during it and I would be in there too. (I called ahead and asked a lot of questions.) And—there would be a wonderful reward if he completed it. He nodded yes and I scheduled the evaluation.

"You will need to finish the evaluation and not walk out to get the reward. Can you do that?"

"Yes."

He slumped in the front seat of the car, his iPod earphones in as usual, as we drove there a few weeks later for the evaluation. When he was a toddler, Lee clung to me in public and at birthday parties refused to leave my lap. As he grew older, I felt distant from him. He rarely started a conversation and usually gave one-word answers to my questions. There was no affection like hugging or saying "I love you."

The autism specialist, a psychologist, had read the multitudes of school and medical records we'd provided and now would test him with a verbal interview. Lee slid down into a comfortable sofa and I sat a few feet away from him. I wished he was young enough to hold on my lap.

"Can you hear me through the iPod, Lee?" the psychologist asked. Lee nodded yes. She said the music would help him focus and supported that. None of his teachers did.

She asked yes or no questions, and he nodded or shook his head while looking down at his iPod the entire time. After an hour we took a break, came back in, and she told us both her diagnosis: He had "high-functioning" autism. She said that it was likely a permanent challenge he would need to manage the rest of his life.

"This is no one's fault you have this, Lee, and you are definitely not alone," she said. She told him he could have a great life if he got some different kinds of help. She explained that many people have it and in addition to that, he had good health, intelligence, and family support, things that really matter. She described autism programs in many schools, trained to be sensitive to his needs. She asked if he had any questions.

He shook his head while looking down. Turning to me he said quietly, "Can I get the reward now?"

"Yes, of course. Thank you for staying."

"Okay if we go?" I asked her.

"Yes. I will write my findings in a letter and send it to you. It was wonderful to meet you, Lee. I see much success and happiness in my clients. Good luck to you."

I was impressed with how well she handled him. Calm, straightforward, accepting. She stood up and reached out her hand. "Would you like to shake hands?"

He nodded. He put out a hand and she shook it. He turned to me and said, "Let's go."

We were at an autism center in St. Paul. I got on the highway, drove out of St. Paul and then though Minneapolis into a western suburb, Golden Valley. I pulled into the parking lot of the Animal Humane Society. We had been there a few times just to pet the animals. His first love in the animal world was a golden hamster, Larry, who'd died a few years earlier. Lee had a clear emotional attachment to Larry that he did not show for anyone else. Lee carried him around, missed him when he was away from home, slept with Larry's glass tank next to his bed, even though Larry loudly ran on the wheel all night—which never upset Lee. If Clair and I made noises, however, it did.

Lee had been asking for a rabbit for a long time. I told him no. I'd researched online and rabbits took special care and skills that I was not ready to take on. He did not want another hamster. I tried. Several times.

I parked the car. "Come on, Lee, let's go get your rabbit." It was one of the only times I saw something on his face other than blankness or rage. I saw surprise, shock, happiness, and gratitude, all at once.

"We're not just visiting?"

"No. Ever since Larry died, you wanted a rabbit. You took good care of Larry, and he was like a friend to you, and you can take care of a rabbit now." He was already rushing past me as I talked, into the building. He went right up to the front desk and asked where the rabbits were. I followed him.

He had his heart set on a flop-eared bunny. They had many bunnies but only two flop-eared rabbits. One seemed lethargic but exceptionally beautiful, with soulful eyes and soft gray and white patches of coloring all over.

"I want her."

I gently moved him over to the one I had been watching. Her name was Lucille. She was all white and was playfully tossing the shredded paper up off the floor of her cage, then hopping around with it on her head. I would have chosen her, no doubt about it. She seemed funny and healthy and happy.

"Look at Lucille here," I said. "She is so active and playful. I am afraid the other one is old or maybe not well. She is not moving around much."

"I don't care—I want this one."

I checked the card of the rabbit he wanted. No name. She was found abandoned in a barn where bales of hay were sold. A young couple came to get hay for their horse, and this rabbit was hiding in it. They took her home and tried to keep her but had to bring her to the Humane Society two weeks later. I took a few deep breaths and let him have the one he wanted. I asked the front desk about her health and they said the veterinarian said she was all clear and handed us the report. It said she was healthy.

The rabbit was estimated to be about four years old. We went into a separate room with her and he tried to hold her but she did not want to be held. She resisted, so he gently put her on the floor. She thumped her leg loudly after he set her down. Rabbits are prey animals, and they thump when they feel threatened so as to seem bigger and scarier. The volunteer who was helping us explained the rabbit would let Lee hold her at home as soon as she felt more comfortable with him. He accepted that and then lay on the floor eye-to-eye with her.

"Hi Thumper," Lee said. "We won't return you like they did. You found your forever home."

It turned out Thumper had an undiagnosed medical condition that became a life-threatening emergency two months after we brought her home. This explained her lethargy. It cost almost a thousand dollars to save her life. She had a gastrointestinal obstruction, not uncommon in rabbits. She spent the night in an animal emergency room. We stayed up all night waiting for the call that would tell us whether she would live or not. At 4:00 a.m. they finally called to say Thumper had turned the corner and would be fine. We could pick her up at 7:00 a.m. Lee suggested that he'd known all along that she was ill and would have died if he had not chosen her.

I called Lee's school before we left to get Thumper, to explain why our son would not be there that day. His special education teacher scoffed. "You should have just gotten a replacement rabbit. He needs to face reality."

I explained our son's history with his hamster, and his brand-new diagnosis, but he had made his judgment and cut me off. He worked only with "oppositional" middle-schoolers and believed in discipline. The following day, Lee had a major upset when he returned to school, refusing to attend class and swearing at that teacher. I am sure there was no empathy or understanding from him. Even if I was being overly protective, I thought he could have been more respectful and polite to Lee. I worried about how my son was being treated there. When the teacher put Lee on the special education bus after his outburst, he told the driver (a young woman who was Lee's only friend so far, after three weeks in the school) not to talk to him at all. I called to withdraw Lee from that school.

After Thumper healed, she was livelier. She had free rein on the main floor of our house. She was house-trained and would go to the bathroom in her crate. She became a welcome addition to our family. Lee brought her to my chambers a few times, to show her off, and my staff and close colleagues came in to meet her. Seeing Lee with Thumper, socializing with adults, gave me great joy.

Now when Lee had a serious negative reaction to something, instead of screaming and breaking things, he took Thumper under a blanket with him. He even told us, through Thumper, what he needed, like, "Thumper is hungry," or "Thumper is mad." This worked, but not forever.

Two years later, when Lee was thirteen, despite having Thumper, he sank into depression. Adolescence with no school yet that worked for him combined to make life overwhelming. And our family was going through a big change: Clair and I had decided to separate, and we sold our boys' childhood home, which caused them all sadness. Even though the separation was amicable—we shared keys and bank accounts and were not rushing to file for divorce—I am sure this disruption affected all three of them deeply and caused Lee pain even though he never spoke of it directly.

I rented a house a few blocks from Common Ground, the meditation center I'd joined and went to almost every day. It had been seven years since I'd had cancer, and I was immersed in meditation, and writing and healing programs, and it seemed to me that Clair was not interested in what I was doing and not interested in changing himself. We were living separate lives most of the time, even when we lived together.

In more than fifteen years Clair and I had tried three marriage counselors, but I saw no improvement. I felt that I was caring for the children mostly by myself because he was tired and on the computer at home most of the time. Finally, a constant irritant for me, however petty it may sound, is that Clair would not eat what I considered healthy food—vegetables, salad, herbs, and spices. He would eat nothing other than his standard diet of pizza, cheeseburgers, spaghetti (sauce from a can only), macaroni and cheese, meat and potatoes with gravy, and many bottles of Coca-Cola per day along with candy, donuts, and ice cream. I wished he could enjoy my cooking the way my boys and my friends at the meditation center did (I was known for providing excellent vegetarian fare for retreats and community events). His ability to look fit and have no health problems made me jealous and angry. I was lonely. Maybe he was, too.

After two years of separation, it was clear Clair had become depressed, and he asked me for help. The boys no longer wanted to go to his apartment (Lee went only a few times in the beginning). It was unkempt, and he never cooked.

He called me one night at 1:00 a.m. and asked if he could live with me and the boys in the house I was renting, in the basement if necessary. I could hear how desperate and hurting he was. I agreed he could move in if he would get professional help right away. He needed inpatient hospital care for clinical depression, took a medical leave from work, and got all new medications. We reconciled our marriage. A few years later we bought our home on the lake. Seeing him suffering in the hospital helped release most of my irritations with him. When the stakes are high, the normal small things in life fall to the bottom of your list.

Before Clair went through his depression and moved back, I switched Lee to an in-home tutor program through the school, which he loved. The teacher came once a week, and later became a support not just for Lee but for our whole family. We are still connected with her and with her daughters and grandchildren.

Every Thursday I took Lee to work with me to get him out of the house. We went out into the community with my new traveling traffic court, each week visiting a different community center for court. Then we had lunch with my friendly staff at local restaurants. Lee loved interesting food. My law clerk, a former special education teacher, would give him documents to sort and talked to him. She had a gift for engaging with him.

But nothing seemed to help for long. One evening Lee was under the blanket with Thumper in a corner of the living room. He had been withdrawn for the past few days. I took a chance and gently crawled under with them and petted Thumper the same way Lee was.

"How is Thumper tonight?"

"Thumper wants to kill herself."

I did not say anything but panicked inside. I waited.

"Thumper wants to go back to the hospital," he said. "It is the only place she feels safe."

This made me sad and confused, but I took him to the emergency room of the children's hospital and he was admitted. I wished his home felt safe to him, like it did for the rest of us. Another level of care was needed. After Lee came home from the hospital, I worried constantly. For three long years, things got worse before they got better.

BENEATH THE MASK

EXPERTS ADVISED US TO DO the following to control Lee's aggressive behaviors: drug him when he was two years old. Call the police when he acted up at age five. Never bring him back to school when he threw a chair in second grade. Transfer him to a restrictive school in third grade and lock him in a classroom. Put him in an institution when he was ten. Place him in a restraint hold at home when he got destructive. Keep him in his room. Mainstream him in seventh grade. Advance him to high school when he kicked out a window in seventh grade. Hospitalize him. Homeschool him. Have police arrest him. Let him suffer the consequences of his behavior and go to juvenile hall. Protect him from his behaviors with a personal care attendant (bodyguard) twenty-four hours a day. Drug him more. Take away all his food until he obeyed—not just snacks and treats but all food and nutrition.

We followed some of the advice, like giving him prescription medicine for anxiety—not at two years old, but when he turned seven. We held the bedroom door shut with him inside in a "time-out" like they advised, and he tipped over a heavy dresser and then threw everything that he could lift out the window into the next-door neighbor's yard. Since this was dangerous, we had to stop him. Clair was trained to restrain him the moment he started damaging things, but as he tried to get Lee into the therapeutic restraint as instructed, Lee bit him all across his chest. We called

911 and said we had a mental health crisis and paramedics came. Several times as a result of these calls, he was hospitalized, and they adjusted his medications and provided counseling, but nothing worked. When he was in the hospital, we got a respite from taking care of him, but it was overshadowed by knowing he was not getting better. Things always went back to the way they had been. We reported the psychologist who had advised us to starve our son to the state board of psychology.

When we called the police the first time, as Lee's psychologist insisted we do, the officers who came laughed at us. A prosecutor dad with huge biceps and a family-court-judge mother? So the kid waved a baseball bat around, twisted the new mini-blinds, and scratched up the leather sofa: It was our fault for not disciplining him. I told Lee's psychologist that we were humiliated, and she said we should have called 911 again and again until we got a decent police officer. Ask for the sergeant. To do what? I wondered. What was the point? This was to teach him to stop being aggressive, I guess. The police would come and he would have to behave thereafter. But consequences made no difference to him. Once, when we said he had to stop playing video games, he brought every single electronic item he owned and piled them in the living room and placed all his games on top. He looked triumphant. We felt we had lost again. Once I took a few hours off work to watch a Dr. Phil episode on uncontrollable children and how to help them: He advocated long timeouts. We had to quit putting Lee in timeout because he would urinate on our beautiful hardwood floors. When a parent asked Dr. Phil about this, afraid her child would do just that, Dr. Phil said, *No child ever did such a thing*. But our son did it every time. I turned off the television and went back to work.

In second grade, after Lee threw the chair, I called the teacher to apologize—no one had gotten hurt—and she begged me to never bring him back. Of course that's not legal. The social worker then sent him to a school with children almost twice his age and size. He learned worse behaviors there. We got a bill

for over sixteen thousand dollars for the independent contractor therapists the school hired without our knowledge. Had we
known, we could have hired the best therapists in the city and
paid them ourselves.

When Lee was seven years old, I was going through breast
cancer radiation, and my chest was red, burned, and hurt to be
touched. After I grounded him for something, he grabbed that
burned skin and twisted it. I cried off and on for hours. Not just
from the physical pain. I worried he had no compassion or feelings. That's when we started him on medication. It broke my
heart. Yet only a month earlier, when I went to get my head
shaved during chemo, he'd demanded to go along. As the hairdresser brought up the razor, he placed his beloved "bunnies"
quilt over my shoulders. It was handmade just for him by a dear
friend of mine, and it showed a house with colorful bunnies in
every window.

The hairdresser trimmed and fitted my wig. I was in shock
seeing myself like this, artificial looking, puffy, and frightened.
But the "bunnies" were around me and for a moment I saw Lee's
heart. The minute we walked in the house, he pulled the wig off
my head and threw it up into the dining room light fixture, laughing. I left it there and went to bed.

Despite the few moments of connection we sometimes shared,
I worried about his future, especially about him being violent
when he grew older.

Once he tried to jump out of my moving car and I pulled over
and called for help. That time, I got a paramedic who hog-tied
our son's hands behind his back, threw him face-down on the
gurney in his ambulance, injected him with an adult dose of Haldol, and said, "I wish I had a Taser to shoot him."

Lee yelled horrible things about wishing the paramedic were
dead and called him names, and the paramedic wrote every single word in the report. There are documented cases of people
suffocating from being turned face down with the weight of a
police officer sitting on top of them. I've never heard of a para-

medic doing that to a juvenile. He seemed to take everything Lee said, an eleven-year-old with special needs, personally. Lee had a seizure from the Haldol. His hands shook for two days. Before it wore off, he called me and said *I love you, Mom* for the first and only time in his life.

I spoke several times with the head of the paramedic department to file a complaint, and he explained they had a standing order to shoot out-of-control adults with Haldol. They had no right to give it to our son, much less an adult dose. He admitted the wrongdoing and apologized. I could have done more, legally speaking, but we were so busy taking care of Lee that we dropped it.

What worked: adopting the bunny after he got evaluated for autism, quitting the therapist who advised police involvement. Taking him out of the schools where he was upset constantly by sensory overload and bringing "homebound" school tutoring into our home, along with an exceptionally kind, retired special education tutor.

Allowing him to *be*.

I let him watch his movies, play his games, eat his foods. I waited patiently for him to feel safe. To find his way through. At times he was more peaceful and more responsive. Other times he went on rampages, like when he wrote with permanent marker on our living room walls because I said he could not go to a heavy metal concert alone at age twelve.

We adopted him at four months old and got no family background on him whatsoever. We knew he had a caring and gentle foster mother from the day he was born until the day he was placed in my arms. She sent an album full of pictures, including a professional photo of him propped up regally on a white fleece background.

When he was young, we tried enrolling him in T-ball, football, hockey, karate. He would try once, then not go back. He ended school at fifteen and got his GED without studying. He knew the law required any person taking the GED to be nineteen years old, but he found an exception, which allowed him to take it at a younger age—if he had medical reasons. He brought all this information to me; then we sent in his diagnostic letter and a supportive letter from the school counselor, and he was approved to take the test. Lee did not want to be a drop-out, and his motivation to do this was encouraging and gave Clair and me hope.

Teachers and therapists often accused us of faulty parenting. Sometimes in defensive mode, I pointed out that our twins, just eighteen months younger, had also been adopted and had none of these behaviors. They were compliant with school rules and cooperative and loving at home. They had dozens of friends and were great at team sports, excelling in soccer.

We went like this, off and on, until Lee was sixteen. One hundred-eighty pounds. Thick black hair to his shoulders. Living in our new home on the lake in a mostly white neighborhood.

I now saw a life coach instead of a therapist. She'd grown up with a sister with profound special needs and extreme behaviors. When Clair and I were separated, she even came to my home sometimes when Lee was out-of-control screaming at me and I needed support. He never accepted her but I got what I needed to keep going. Kindness and understanding. One time, I stayed late at my appointment at her office and got home after the time I had told him. When I walked in, he announced, "I am going to move to Korea and you will never see me again!"

I stared at him and he stared back. I erupted into sobs as I imagined him leaving. When I paused, he made that rare eye contact with me and said, "Now you know how I feel."

This was the beginning of my understanding of his viewpoint and his wounds. Another time I was at a coaching session, and I knew Clair would be home before me, so I did not worry too much about running over the time. When I came out, there were thirteen messages from Clair. Lee had acted up, and my husband had called the police.

I was listening to the voice messages as I raced home. Lee had grabbed two French knives and stood on the front steps waiting for the police.

It was dusk. I only got through a few of the voice messages but in one Clair's voice was shaking as he told me he called the police and Lee threatened that he would make them kill him. Lee and Clair were outside waiting.

Clair had told the 911 operator that Lee had knives.

The police pulled up, started up the walk, and Clair said to the officers, "He has knives."

One of the officers said in a calm voice, "Yes, we know."

The officer looked at Lee and said quietly, gently, "What's the matter, buddy?"

Lee began sobbing and dropped the knives. The officer put his arm around him and asked if he could help. Lee nodded yes. The officer asked if he could take him to the hospital to get help.

Lee nodded again. The officer gave him a choice to ride with his dad or with him. He chose Dad.

The police officer said he would follow them to make sure he was okay and got there safely and Lee nodded again. The officer walked into the psych ER with Lee and shook his hand and wished him all the best.

When I got to that voicemail, the one where they were escorted to the hospital by the police, I changed course and raced to the hospital. I called Clair, who said Lee didn't want to see me. I could not stay away. I walked into the hospital room and quietly sat in the corner, and he seemed to accept me.

A teenager now, he was too old for the children's hospital. Instead, he was admitted into the adolescent psychiatric ward. The on-call therapist came to talk to us and I was instantly impressed with her. She was different from the others. Lee listened to her and talked directly with her, which was rare. When he was young, he used to look at me so that I would speak for him, like an interpreter. Afterward I asked her where she got the skills to deal with someone like him, and she said she used to have a mobile community counseling service, going into homes even when a fight was happening between a teenager and a parent, even when someone was suicidal.

I told her our history in our private meeting and about all the experts we had been through, none of whom had helped him. Now he was hoping the police would shoot him. I couldn't help putting my head down and sobbing on the table.

She gently laid a hand on my arm and let me cry.

"We won't hurt or drug him, Sue. I see an intelligent, gifted child." We said goodbye to Lee, relieved that he was in good hands.

If not for that kind police officer, Lee might have died. I always wanted to find out the name of the officer to thank him, but I never did. There was no written report. I have sent him gratitude from my heart often for treating our son like a hurting person, and not reacting to him with violence.

I called Children's Home Society, the adoption agency that arranged all three of our international adoptions, and got a counselor who listened to my whole story. Let me cry. Waited patiently to speak.

Then she told me about the book *Beneath the Mask* written by Debbie Riley with John Meeks for adoptive parents. Riley is a therapist and also an adoptive parent of a special needs internationally adopted child. I read the whole book in one evening. One of the main themes was that adopted children, especially when they are teenagers, feel they must project love for their adoptive parents even if they do not feel it and maybe never did. They know their parents would be crushed, and it becomes their darkest secret.

Many of them do not want to be here. They wish to be back home in their home country. Yet if they go back, they would be considered American, would not be able to speak the language, and would not fit in.

Riley titled her book *Beneath the Mask* because these deep feelings are real and often hidden behind a mask of feigned "I love you's." Or in Lee's case, behind anger raging forth and only one drug-induced "I love you." I'd had no idea. The book opened my eyes to his world view.

Riley also contends that adopted teens are over-pathologized and most therapists completely overlook the adoption and its effect. Ours did.

At the C.A.S.E. Center, which Riley co-founded, adopted teens make art masks. They shape clay to their faces, then paint and decorate them. When the masks are finished, they hold them up to their faces. Then they remove the masks, and tell their stories with their true faces exposed—stories of feeling different, feeling rejected, and sometimes not feeling love for their adoptive parents. They feel safe enough there to talk about what is under those masks. For the first time in their lives, their painful feelings are normalized and accepted.

I prepared myself to be open to whatever Lee wanted or needed to tell us, come what may. Clair and I arrived at the hospital for a special meeting, a family session—Lee and the counselor were waiting for us.

We walked in. Sat across from Lee. He was leaning over his knees, his head down, hands on forehead, his hair hanging like a thick black curtain over his entire face.

"Lee has something to tell you." The counselor gave me a penetrating look. Like "Hold on, Mom."

"Good. We are here to listen." My heart pounded but I pretended to be calm.

"Okay," she said. "Remember you said you would tell them what you told me. I encourage you to tell them because this will help you feel even better. Do you still agree?"

He nodded his head slightly.

"Okay," she said. "Go ahead when you are ready."

We sat in silence. My heart was still pounding, and I tried to focus on my breath. Clair tried to hold my hand but I pulled away. I wanted to focus only on Lee.

His muffled voice spoke. "I don't want to be here. With you and the twins. You are not my family. I did not want to come here to the US I hate everything here. I want to move to a group home and start over without you."

It seemed so hard for him to say and I was proud of him for doing it. It all made sense now.

Just like the teenagers in the masks, he was hiding all these years the fact that he did not love us the way we loved him, or even at all, and he could not tell us. This was not a pathology, like all the other therapists had suggested. He was suffering real pain. From being taken from his homeland and birth family to a new country without any choice. Taken away from a solid and loving caregiver, the only one he knew for his first four months after being born. I always thought he was lucky to have her, but it turns out this also led to a tragic separation. His feelings were completely understandable, especially as a teenager trying to find his own identity.

I saw Clair looking shocked and sad, and I was sure he wanted to jump in and say what the book said not to: "*Oh, but we love you so much! We are your family, and we will take care of you.*"

He had not read the book and I could not explain all this to him. I put my finger to my lips to signal Clair not to say anything.

"Thank you for telling us," I said. "I am really glad you did. So honest and courageous. Many kids can't tell their parents they don't love them the way we love you. You didn't ask to be taken out of your country, your home. Away from your loving foster mother, Mrs. Lim. You didn't ask to come here. You woke up one day in a different country. You had no voice in the matter."

I paused.

"Well, now you do. Please know we understand and will work with you and your counselor to find a place where you feel comfortable." I did not like saying that but took comfort in knowing it was the right thing. It was what he needed.

He did not say a word for several minutes. It seemed like he was taking this in. He could tell the truth and we would listen. We would support his wishes, help him find his way back "home" wherever that was. We loved him without conditions.

With a sweeping motion, he sat up and his shoulder length hair was airborne, following the arc of his moving head until he was sitting tall, with his hair fully back and off his forehead, all of it flowing down his back. We saw his full face, which was rare. He looked at me directly, and instead of flatness, I saw life in his eyes.

"When can I get out of here? Can we get Chipotle on the way home?"

His counselor smiled and said she could get the paperwork started to discharge him from the hospital and trusted we would continue to work together to help Lee. He looked at her and nodded yes. I hugged her tight before she left. I found out later she had spent hours talking to him, supporting him that whole day before we arrived. My admiration for her is as alive today as if that session just happened this afternoon.

I packed up his clothes while Clair brought the car around. The three of us went to the Chipotle near the hospital. Normally we never ate together because Lee ate alone in his room. We never, ever went to restaurants together.

We all got an abundant meal. He talked baseball with his dad and asked me about getting a ticket to a concert by A Perfect Circle, who were coming to Minneapolis. He was sixteen. That was his last hospitalization.

V

___

Putting My Heart into the Body of Family Law

My SIMPLE IDEA TO REDUCE the animosity and adversarial nature of family court was this: Instead of making the parties watch an educational film and listen to a short talk from a family court judge, I would meet them personally, privately, in chambers. I would tell them the truth.

I wrote a personal, signed-in-ink letter to parents saying I would waive the generic auditorium movie and judge-talk requirement if they chose to meet with me to satisfy the educational requirement. They all chose to meet with me.

It caused a stir among the family bar association and some members of the court that I would meet with people who had filed for divorce without their lawyers present. I pointed out the law to them, which requires the court to "educate parents about the impact that divorce, the restructuring of families, and judicial proceedings have upon children and families; methods for preventing parenting time conflicts; and dispute resolution options."

These meetings were not mandatory—people were offered a choice of the personal meeting with me instead of the movie and talk. One of the most vocal and aggressive family court attorneys wrote me a letter stating she would not allow her client to attend the meeting without her. I said she was welcome to join us. Afterward, she told the concerned attorneys on the bar association's family law committee that there was nothing to worry about: We did not discuss the case, and I just informed them of the road that lay ahead.

I told the parents that 95 percent of all cases settle without a trial. Unfortunately, the court was set up to move everything toward trial. This was costly and stressful, and it forced parents to go to battle against one another. At this point, quite a few had tears or cried, saying, "I was the child of a divorce. I never felt like anyone cared about my feelings or what I needed. I never want to do that to my children."

It was clear most parents are capable of making the best decisions about their children and finances, and yet, as I told them, I would never meet their children, I had no degree in psychology, and if they went to trial, I would be given the authority to decide what was in their children's best interests. If one parent disagreed with my ruling, this could go to the court of appeals and take years and tens of thousands of dollars to resolve.

When I started the pilot project on my new cases, I realized I needed a flow chart. I called the head of family court administration.

"How do these files get on my desk?" I asked. "What is the flow chart for parents from the time their lawyer files their case until trial? I want to contact them the moment they file their divorce."

"There is no flow chart," she said. Then she quickly added, "No problem. I will make a quick-and-dirty flow chart and e-mail it to you."

What I received was exactly what I needed. Dozens of boxes of various sizes, with arrows going every which way, entirely filled an 8 1/2 x 11" sheet of paper. It looked like a board game gone off-kilter. There was even a box labeled "Case in Limbo."

I enlarged the chart and printed it on a four-by-three-foot board. I placed this behind my desk, leaning it against the wall, until the proper time. When I showed parents they were at the

first box labelled "Start Here" and could avoid all the other procedures and costs if they settled now rather than wait until the
eve of trial, they nodded. I told them about mediation. To make
it easier for them, I had a mediator standing by in a conference
room next door to my chambers. It took weeks to get permission
to use that office one day a week but I got it. I brought in framed
poster art by Toulouse-Lautrec for the walls, a rug to put over the
old carpet, a few lamps, and a bowl of chocolates on the round
table. The mediator, trained in transformative mediation, even
gave them the choice to not listen to him and told them they were
free to leave at any time. Every step of the process was designed
to allow choice, to empower the parents.

That is just what happened. Ninety-eight percent of the cou-
ples chose an alternative to court. After I published these dramatic results, many lawyers, judges, and mediators wanted to hear
more, and I was invited to speak at statewide judicial conferences,
to the bar association, and at an international conference on
transformative mediation.

Then, instead of adopting this tried-and-true method, as I
expected, the court hired a consultant from Texas. He "inter-
viewed" me for ten minutes in my chambers and did not ask a
single question. I felt he was not listening to me. Then he brought
a group of judges and administrators to a conference in Texas. I
was not invited.

The court personnel came back with a "Case Management
Conference" form, which was another legal document to file.
Parents were now required to appear in court within three weeks
of filing their divorce rather than the case languishing indefinitely
(an improvement), but attorneys were once again involved from
the beginning. There was no change to the required educational
component. They failed to see (or chose not to see) that the parents needed to be empowered, not told what to do or sent to more
experts to evaluate their case.

I was crushed they were unable to institute change in the personal way I'd envisioned, but I was grateful the court and the

public became aware that even one *temporary* hearing caused *permanent* damage. There was no denying this anymore. No one, not even lawyers, could simply call and get a hearing date as they could when I began on the bench.

As the years went on, I still handled my cases differently, and not long before I retired because the cancer had returned, I was criticized for "not closing cases fast enough." I met with the heads of administration and family court and acknowledged I did things differently and noted that I had invited them to observe, but they never had. They were fixated on the speed factor, it seemed to me, as if these families' lives were on a conveyor belt.

I recall the time a divorced couple appeared on a "post-decree" matter, because the mother wanted to move to Arizona where her new husband had a new job. The ex-husband refused to agree, because he would not see his two sons every week or be a part of their daily activities anymore. The case was set for trial, with the parents representing themselves.

I came into the courtroom and made a few inquiries to see if there was a chance of settlement. I noticed the man had on a dark suit and tie, and the woman had on a brightly colored head wrap and long colorful dress. As we talked, I saw a group of people in similar traditional African dress, peering in the small window on the locked courtroom door. I asked who they were and was told they were the couple's Liberian extended family.

After more discussion, the parents agreed the extended family should be part of the conversation and might even help them make an agreement. The room suddenly filled with about fifteen to twenty adults of varying ages, in their colorful clothing, and one gentleman wearing an ornately embroidered red kufi hat who seemed to be the eldest and the facilitator.

I left them gathered around the long counsel table. It was late morning and they would likely work into lunchtime. A law clerk and I raced to the local grocery store where I bought multiple party-sized fruit trays. We returned, quietly set up the food, many types of tea, hot water, plates, and cups, and then left again.

I looked in a few times over the next few hours and saw that the fruit and tea were untouched, but the family members were around the table; it seemed to me like they were having a peaceful discussion.

About an hour later, there was a knock on our door and we were told that they had an agreement. I came in with our court reporter to make it official and noticed every piece of fruit was gone and everyone had a teacup in their hand. The elder gentleman in the red kufi took the witness stand and read their agreement, and both parties agreed on the record to abide by it. The mother could move to Arizona with the children, but she would pay to have them visit their father one weekend every month in Minnesota. The father could visit them any time in their new home, at his expense. It was not ideal for him, because it disrupted his routine with the boys, but he said it would work.

As they were leaving, chatting with one another, no one mentioned the fruit or said "thank you." I am embarrassed to admit I wondered if they thought all courts provided heathy snacks during settlement discussions. But just as I had that thought, one of the last people to file out, an older woman, turned around, smiled, and said, "We thank you for the fruit. Look, we ate it all!" She waved her arm at the empty trays, laughed heartily, and left.

How could I tell the bureaucrats and traditional judges that I felt obligated to focus on what the people needed first and not how fast I could close their case? If parents needed phone conferences or extra hearings or just extra time to tell their stories, I gave that to them. I tried to provide whatever they needed. I was sure that if we allowed people to get to the root of their problems, they would not need to keep coming back frequently, as so many did.

Some people had mental health issues, some had anger and abuse issues, others were addicted to drugs. I tried to meet them where they were, even if they were loud or angry or fearful. Some clerks understood my methods and others wished I would "control things." I found that people responded well when I allowed them to be themselves or just acknowledged their suffering.

One time, when two parents came into my courtroom, I felt I was needed simply to witness their pain. They'd had three children together, and he'd remarried. Their teenaged son had recently hanged himself. The man and the woman sat at opposite ends of the long table in front of me like most divorcing people in court naturally do.

I said, "I am so sorry about the loss of your son." The mother pulled the tissue box closer and stared down at it.

The father looked away. Then he said, "She's a good mother. A *great* mother." He glanced at the woman, then away. "I had to do this. I wanted to help her out." The woman turned toward him, almost in slow motion.

"Help me out?" she said. "Sending the sheriff to my door? With papers saying I'm unfit? How does this help me out? How could you do this to me?"

He looked only at me. "The lady downstairs said to fill in the blanks, then the sheriff has to serve it because it is an emergency," he said. "I told the lady this would upset her. She said, 'It's the law. You have to put this in writing to the court if you think your children are not being taken care of.'"

The woman still faced him, not me. The man continued speaking to me. "The kids say she doesn't get out of bed. They're missing too much school. Their hair and clothes are dirty. The school social worker threatened to put them in foster care or file for truancy if I didn't do this."

"The *sheriff*." She never removed her gaze from him.

He looked at her for the first time and said, "The school and I call you, but you never answer."

"You have no idea," she said. "How hard this is. The little ones. They were there. They saw him like that."

"I know, baby, I know. But we can't lose them too."

"Look at you," she said. "Acting like nothing happened. Your new suit. Your big job. New wife and baby. You *don't* know. I've got nothing. Nothing but reminders. Finding him. Like that."

Slowly, one by one, she pulled out three tissues. She squeezed them inside her fist.

"I do think of him," the father said. "Everything reminds me of him," he said, his voice breaking. He dropped his head into his hands, sobbing. Then he got up and moved over to the chair next to her, grabbed some tissues, and wiped his face. He placed his arm over her shoulders. They bowed their heads close, whispering.

After a few minutes, I wondered what to do, so I quietly asked, "Would you like us to give you a few moments to yourselves?" The mother shook her head "no" without looking up.

"No," the father said. "Please don't go."

It was already past the time for calling the next case. I was well aware of that. I saw my clerk's questioning looks on my left and the large clock on the right. I tried to breathe slowly and stay aware of my feet on the floor, hoping to get grounded. I was in unknown territory. The father looked at me.

"We're all going to start grief counseling," he said. "She has the name of a good counselor. I'll go to her place every morning, get the kids ready for school, then come back and make dinner, help with homework, give the kids their baths, and put them to bed."

He looked at the woman. "My wife will understand. My boss will understand. We're all in this together. I am not taking them away from you. Do you believe me?"

She nodded. He pushed the papers toward me.

"How do I stop all this?" he asked me. "Can you just throw these away? This is not at all what I wanted." I said I would dismiss the case, and I could shred those papers if he wanted me to.

He pulled them back. "No. I just realized. I want to tear them up myself."

The two of them stood and turned to the door. With an arm

firmly around each other's waist, as if holding each other up, they left the courtroom.

If I had opened the hearing with the traditional legal process, I would have said, "I see you are filing for a change of custody and your papers have established the grounds to set this for trial. Ma'am, I am sorry but you can't refute these allegations today, but will be able to at a trial."

I doubt that an opening like that would have led to this kind of agreement.

Every day, almost all of my cases held pain and suffering, love and hate. Often people found their way to court because they felt they had no other choices. None was offered to them.

Although my methods seemed inappropriate and even impossible to those with a traditional, institutional mindset, parents and families usually found my courtroom a safe space to communicate and work out their problems.

When the cancer returned, it was hard to leave permanently; I knew I had a lot more work to do. The innovations I had made years earlier weren't enough. I saw many more changes I wanted to make, like providing a compassionate court representative to meet people as soon as they came in the door of family court, seeing what was needed and providing it immediately. I felt confident I could help before my condition got worse. I wanted us to be like the Mayo brothers, whose mission statement in creating the first Mayo Clinic was "the needs of the patient come first." I'd scheduled a meeting with my family court colleagues to brainstorm my ideas before submitting them, but the judge in charge of family court stopped in my chambers laughing and saying she had "shanghaied" my meeting away from me. She brought in a retired judge as a consultant and ran the meeting herself. Unfortunately, she created a stifling and drawn-out application process for anyone who wanted to implement changes. She would decide everything. My ideas had no chance—which was her goal all along. I still feel regret today, thinking of the lost opportunity for our court to be a model of the most innovative and responsive family court in the nation.

There is a Buddhist teaching about changes being incremental: Sometimes they do not bear fruit for a long time, maybe not even in our own lifetime, but we need to keep practicing anyway. One drop in the bucket at a time, one moment of mindfulness, and some day, sometime in the future, the bucket will overflow. We will get there if we keep practicing. One drop at a time.

When I sobered up, I was still miserable, yet the group applauded my sobriety, telling me to live one day at a time, trusting I was "sowing seeds that would bear fruit someday." Maybe I was just throwing seeds on the family court's concrete plaza, a place where seeds would never take hold, but I hoped maybe just one seed would sprout up through a crack somewhere in the concrete.

Nowadays, I practice what I call "patient waiting," a practice that has been helpful to me many times with my cancer treatments and with my family, as I watch my three sons become independent young men.

Pablo Casals, possibly the greatest cellist of all time, was asked why he continued to practice three hours a day at the age of ninety-four. He replied, "I am beginning to see some improvement."

POINTILLISM AND
PUBLIC SPEAKING

I KNOW I AM HARDLY alone in dreading public speaking. For me, a survivor of selective mutism and social phobia, it was always an anxious struggle. Often I would get a backache so painful I needed to find a private spot and lie on the floor before a legal talk because I could barely stand. Afterward, I was exhilarated. This surprised me every time.

When asked to give a talk, I worked very hard on it. Preparation gave me confidence; then I would try to deliver the material in a relaxed voice and manner. In 2014, I had less than an hour before I had to give the most personal and meaningful talk of my life, and I was completely blocked.

I'd been asked to co-design an international symposium by a colleague who did not yet know that my cancer had metastasized. He did not know I had a brain tumor that was considered inoperable. It had been radiated, but it did not shrink or disappear. The treatment only made me tired and groggy.

The symposium was supported by the Fetzer Institute and would bring fifty leaders and innovators from all over the world to Minneapolis to discover how compassion could be brought into family law and the courts. We called it "Divorce: What's Love Got to Do With It?"

I met my colleague for lunch, told him about the cancer, and said yes, I would be his co-chair and help design the event. It was a dream of my entire professional life coming true, to spread the message of incorporating kindness and compassion in family law to a global audience.

On opening night, I was to speak about the origins of the symposium, my involvement, and my hopes for the outcome. I would be the last speaker.

I wanted my talk to be clear, focused, and very short. I wanted to counteract the dullness and fatigue I felt most of the time. I had notes and outlines and "mind-maps," but no single theme was emerging. My life seemed too complex, my dreams too large, and I lacked the clarity of a unifying principle. I brought reams of notes to the conference center hotel room and trusted I would pull something together. Speaking to fifty world leaders from law, psychology, mediation, medicine, and mindfulness was intimidating.

An hour before my scheduled talk, I was in my hotel room, pacing, talking out loud, trying to find an opening line, my papers spread all over the bed. I wanted to tell my life story, abbreviated of course, and explain how I was led to this transformative work. I wanted to share some of the hardships and challenges I faced, so that everyone at the conference would feel welcome—not just their intellects but all parts of them: wounded or imperfect; personal, not just professional.

Suddenly I saw it. From the depths of my French major over forty years earlier came the art concept of "pointillism." Not a PowerPoint—far from it. I would imagine a blank canvas and then paint a spot for each experience that seemed important—a dab of bright color for each one. I trusted the audience would be able to see the "whole" when I was done.

I felt great. Excited and creative. Then I made a mistake right before I went downstairs for the opening ceremony. In a moment of doubt about my brain function and memory, I looked up pointillism in Wikipedia: "The term pointillism was first coined by art critics in the late 1880s to ridicule the works of these artists."

I was crushed. I'd thought it was a serious genre. But before I slammed my computer shut, I saw a solution.

As I spoke to the crowd, I told them how I came up with the idea to use pointillism as my "form" for the talk, which brought back good memories of being a French major and my time in France, and then I told them my mistake of looking it up in Wikipedia.

"I was feeling good about coming up with this idea, which even tied in with my passion for France," I said. "But when I doubted my brain and my memory, I ran back to check Wikipedia, and learned pointillism was ridiculed by art critics." The crowd laughed. "I scrolled further and saw Vincent Van Gogh, his famous self-portrait done in pointillism, and figured if it was good enough for him, it was good enough for me."

I proceeded to talk about how I came to be co-chair of this symposium and what moved me to take on the entire institution of family court to make it more inclusive and compassionate—transforming it into a place that treated everyone with dignity. I said that one of the most important changes looked simple: I met the family right away, before any negative accusations were filed. I welcomed them personally in chambers, with my children's photos on my desk and their drawings on the wall. I didn't have my robe on.

My talk briefly mentioned some of the tragedies from my childhood, like having a brilliant trial lawyer father who became a violent alcoholic. How none of the institutions we had to deal with treated us with dignity when we most needed it: not the Catholic Church (which told my mother she could not divorce Dad even though he was violent), not the welfare department (which had us jump through many hoops and face rude bureaucrats just to get food stamps and a few hundred dollars a month), not the courts (which never enforced the orders against my father). How all of this steered me to wanting to represent the poorest of the poor, the abused, the voiceless.

Then I talked about how I became an alcoholic, even though

I'd sworn I would never drink. How this humbled me. How the folks at AA modeled a way of life that touched me and changed my thinking on everything. It inspired me to "practice these principles in all my affairs," meaning I brought their beautiful program into the courtroom, without anyone knowing. The fellowship of AA accepted me at my worst, and it changed me for the better. I was committed to ensuring everyone received the same kind of acceptance from me. Of course I fell short, but this was always my inner driving principle. I tried each day to create a welcoming family court that empowered but never judged.

The talk turned out well. It seemed that my few, important dabs of color were sufficient. Listeners added whatever they needed, blended the anecdotes into a fuller story and identified with me, I learned afterward. Pointillism became a catchword for the entire symposium and made it possible for us to talk about complex issues artfully. It opened the door for these many-credentialed experts to share their own struggles, which helped them find compassion for those we were there to serve.

I read more about pointillism months after the talk and found out it uses the same optical illusion our printers and televisions use. According to Wikipedia:

> The technique relies on the ability of the eye and mind of the viewer to blend the color spots into a fuller range of tones. . . . Pointillism is analogous to the four-color CMYK printing process used by some color printers and large presses that place dots of cyan [blue], magenta [red], yellow, and key [black]. Televisions and computer monitors use a similar technique to represent image colors using Red, Green, and Blue (RGB) colors.

What may be even more important is the theory that having white space around a dab of color intensifies it, making it more brilliant. I tend to agree with this, after seeing one of the most famous pointillist paintings at the Art Institute of Chicago: Seurat's glowing "A Sunday Afternoon on the Island of La Grande Jatte." Seurat's technique makes the colors stand out and have a vibration I don't see in other paintings.

After my pointillism talk was over, the group broke up, and I stood alone, relieved and exhausted, ready to fall into bed.

Suddenly a woman with short black hair made a beeline across the conference room to get to me. She had tears in her eyes and put both hands on my shoulders. She said she had come to the symposium somewhat out of obligation due to her position. Now she knew she was meant to be there, thanked me, and left. My co-chair told me she was a well-known CEO of an international group. A month after the symposium, the CEO informed us that she and her board of directors had decided to dedicate the entire winter edition of their journal to the symposium. I felt joy hearing this, knowing that it would carry our message around the world.

I even published an article about family court in the journal, entitled "Five Ways to Put a Heart into Family Court." She chose it, despite the objections of some, who claimed the courts were the problem. There are many who believe family court is an "evil empire." But they have never been in my courtroom.

While there are some alternative, out-of-court models, most people can't afford them, because they involve expensive teams of experts—a lawyer for each side, an accountant, a psychologist—which I felt once again continued the problem of portraying the parents as if they could not make their own decisions. My article made the dramatic suggestion that courts could be non-adversarial as well. The Fetzer Institute, committed to raising awareness of love and forgiveness in the workplace, also decided to feature my article on its website. My son Tom, who was about to start art school, did the art for the article, which appeared on the institute's website. He depicted a scale of justice, with a heart on one side and two children on the other side, one arm around each other's waist, the other arms holding onto the chain of the scale of justice like it was a swing.

Afterward, the CEO and I talked by e-mail and phone, read each other's articles for the journal, and became friends. I told her I wanted to fly out to Phoenix just to have lunch or dinner with her. I could use a few days away from my own life. She was amazed I would do that, and we began planning.

Soon after, I was referred to a world-renowned surgeon in Phoenix, known for removing "inoperable" brain tumors. My new friend in Phoenix took care of me throughout the entire process and the two trips—one for the consultation and the other for the surgery. She welcomed Mick and my cousin Kris into her home as well. She cooked for us and took time off from her many responsibilities. The surgeon removed the entire tumor.

We both had childhoods that were extremely difficult. We both dedicated our time to helping others. We both took risks telling our personal stories: me to fifty leaders in the field of family conflict, and she in dedicating an entire journal to love and family law that included personal details of her own childhood story. She overcame unspeakable odds. We both took the risk of showing who we are behind the degrees, honors, and accolades.

I ended my article with this quote from the Dalai Lama: "Be kind whenever possible. It is always possible." It is the second line that raises the bar. This quote forced me out of complacency and helped me make a conscious effort to be kind, even when I was mistreated by colleagues, who showed me I was still reactive and had much room to improve when I thought I was doing pretty well.

Because I was bold enough to end a scholarly legal article for an international journal with the Dalai Lama's kindness quote, I knew that I had made some progress: Like Pablo Casals, I was beginning to see some improvement.

FINDING MY STORY

ONE CHALLENGE I ENCOUNTERED WHILE trying to figure out how to tell my life story started after I began studying Buddhism and attending silent meditation retreats. I learned, especially through the teachings of a popular Buddhist author, that when meditation students feel strong emotions, triggered by a memory, event, or thought, we are supposed to "drop the story line" and just be open to the underlying emotions. I disliked everything about *dropping the story line*. This conflict—me trying to understand the stories of my life, their teaching to drop all my stories—came to a head on a particular retreat. After four days of silent meditation, I was sitting outside the retreat center, meditating under a tree overlooking the calm lake, and started crying. After a time, these words came to me: *What happened to you as a child broke your heart.*

I saw how I'd spent most of my life either trying to pass as "normal" or striving to be exceptional. Too often I'd ignored my broken heart. Covered it up, hid it from the outside world, designed my resumé so no one could find it. I sometimes even tried to hide it from myself. But at that moment, I was alone with my heartache. My pain made sense. I knew why I hurt so much, and I felt it, viscerally, to my core. It was as real as the broken arm I suffered when I was seven years old.

Later that day, in our single fifteen-minute private meeting with my beloved teacher, I was excited to tell her of this discovery. After I did, she said, "Sue, you take everything so personally. Drop the story line. You don't need it here. Just be with the pain."

There it was. I was supposed to be mute again. And I was not supposed to trust my own heart and emotions. I'd been dismissed once again, for being "me." I felt anger rising, then shame for feeling upset with my beloved teacher. I'd spent years unearthing my feelings, and I was supposed to forget all that? To her, it was a "story line," but it was my life. How could I not take it personally? There was a pause in the room, during which I debated a range of responses, from walking out of her small office forever and slamming the door, to saying nothing at all. With my heart beating fast and strong, I chose to speak up. "How can I drop the stories when I am just learning what they are?"

I do not remember her response.

From then on, I chose to continue looking for my stories. I meditated, reflected, and wrote. I went on blind faith that it was important for me to find my stories and to share them, no matter what my teacher said. I sifted through the pieces of my past. As I wrote, it came alive. It wasn't just a story line, it was the texture of my lived experience, the people, the things, and the moments that not only broke my heart but made me who I am. A skeletal father in a cashmere coat. A dying mother calling for me by banging a wooden spoon. An irrepressible talking red poodle, a shiny blue Mustang, a sleek bass guitar. Black-out drunks and a church basement full of welcoming strangers. A photograph of two tiny bundled baby boys. A kind police officer with his arm around the shoulders of a sobbing teenaged boy. A black robe and a courtroom full of other families' confusion and heartache. A doctor's dread pronouncement and a seemingly endless series of scans, radiations, and surgeries. The glittering shards of a broken gavel.

I found out that there were no stories until I began to tell them. But when I did, I made connections among the pieces, I made sense of things. I found my own part, the choices I made, and I came to believe my stories may be useful to others.

Hannah Arendt, the renowned political philosopher, once

said: "The story reveals the meaning of what otherwise would remain an unbearable sequence of sheer happenings." Instead of a litany of unbearable wrongs, I saw a life, and it was mine.

ALREADY BROKEN

KINTSUGI IS AN ANCIENT JAPANESE method of filling in the cracks of broken porcelain with gold. Often the repaired piece is considered more beautiful than the original.

Also known as *Kintsukuroi*, kintsugi translates as "golden joinery." It's linked to the Japanese philosophy of wabi-sabi, which honors the beauty of imperfections. The kintsugi technique emphasizes, rather than hides, what is broken. It embraces the damage as part of the object's history instead of finding it unacceptable, something to be hidden or thrown away. This is the opposite of everything I was taught—I was supposed to be perfect and if I was not, I had to hide all my imperfections. This belief is implicit in our consumer culture: If something is broken, toss it out; if something is flawed, hide it.

Kintsugi is a good metaphor for how I was able to start healing a life that was not only cracked, but broken apart—and, in a few places, shattered beyond recognition. When I suffered from the violence, alcoholism, and poverty in my childhood home, my grandmother's love was the golden joinery that held me together.

Before I found sobriety, I was living two lives in the same mind and body: the smart, quiet, good girl and the blacked-out alcoholic. I had no guidebook to follow, nothing to rely upon, and every day unfolded without me knowing how it would end. The unconditional acceptance I received in the AA program was like golden joinery that helped put me back together.

For most of my life, my greatest wish was to be unbroken. I wanted to be someone else and somewhere else. Further along, doing better. I tried to get rid of the pain in my life and deny it rather than *welcome* it.

When I finally had the courage to look at my brokenness and then show my failures and darkest moments to others—to dear friends, to people in AA meetings, in counseling, and at Commonweal and Common Ground—I received acceptance and was loved just the way I was. Those broken edges were transformed into what students of kintsugi call "precious scars," which honor my whole life. Nothing was hidden or left out.

I also needed to learn unconditional love for myself and not just seek it from outside of me. This was my most difficult challenge, since I felt unlovable most of the time. When I was able to practice love for myself, I found that I could love others and their flaws, even the more challenging people.

Because of kintsugi, I no longer think of my broken parts as wounds—I see them as evidence of my life and evidence of my healing. One of my favorite examples of kintsugi is a small dark green bowl that I saw online. It looked as small as my hand. The golden latticework pools in some areas, filling in the gaps, and thins out in others, stretching through the glaze like a spider's web sparkling in the sun. It is hard to imagine this bowl has ever been shattered; the repair does not look like a repair, but intentional, artful. As if the bowl was meant to be broken and fit back together with gleaming gold, exactly in this pattern, from the moment it was created.

As I look at the pieces of my life, I see the girl in braids playing the piano, writing poems for Mom and Dad, giving life to her stuffed animals. I see the girl with the broken heart who silently kept going, hating her shyness, getting good grades, getting drunk, then getting sober. I see the woman who spent her days in the courthouse with other people's families, trying to assist them in mending their lives. I see her writing stories, and I see her mother, father, brothers, husband, and children.

Now my body is broken. Cancer lives in every bone. Twenty tumors have appeared in my head, now five in my liver. I have long, deep scars on my scalp and titanium inside my skull. I have scars on my chest, side, and back from breast reconstruction and having ports placed in my chest. Some scars are hidden inside my face, half numb from having a pituitary tumor removed. I have been poked with needles for spinal fluid, a liver biopsy, and countless injections and blood draws. Tumors in my brain, breast, and hip have been burned with radiation thirty-four times, and some healthy parts of me were burned in the process.

The final piece is the woman with terminal cancer who wants to stay alive for her loved ones. The woman who will, I hope, let go in peace when death comes. I know that nothing, not even the finest kintsugi, lasts forever. But for now, these pieces are joined together: what I was, what happened, and what I have become. The bowl is more beautiful because it was broken. As an old kintsugi quote says, "The true life of the bowl began the moment it was dropped."

EPILOGUE

MICK COCHRANE

SUE DIED ON SATURDAY, FEBRUARY 13, 2021. She was tucked in her own bed, wearing her favorite pajamas, surrounded by artifacts and mementos of her remarkable life, her "boys" close by. She had entered hospice care only a few days before, maintaining right until the end that remarkable blend of clear-eyed acceptance, scientific and spiritual curiosity, joyful other-directed energy, and optimism she exhibited the entire last decade of her life.

I flew to Minneapolis from Buffalo to be with Sue and her family in those last days. Mostly she slept. When awake, it wasn't easy for her to communicate but she heard and understood what we said, all our expressions of love and gratitude. When she knew I had arrived and that it was me patting her hand, she whispered, "My Mick." Later, when I told her that one of her twins had been outside in 10-below-zero weather with no gloves, Sue, remembering the viral images of Senator Sanders at Joe Biden's inauguration a couple of weeks before, said quietly, "Needs Bernie's mittens." Since her diagnosis, she and I had each read and discussed many books about death and dying and had already said to each other many times over the famous four things recommended by palliative care and hospice experts to bring peace at the end of life: "Please forgive me," "I forgive you," "Thank you," and "I love you." Now, there was nothing more for us to say, nothing more to do except be together.

The afternoon before Sue died, a hospice social worker paid a visit. She gathered us in the living room, took out a notebook, and asked, "So what is Susan like?" Over an hour later, it felt as if we had only scratched the surface. A person who survived a traumatic childhood and brought courage and hope to others. A compassionate seeker of justice for the marginalized. A brilliant student of language. A cutthroat cribbage player. A spiritual seeker and wise woman and bodhisattva. A mom who always believed in her sons and honored their dreams. A lover of cats and all animals. A multi-talented artist, musician—and writer.

Beginning in late 2020, in the middle of the pandemic, when it was not possible for me to visit in person, Sue and I would watch movies together via Zoom, usually one a night, or split over several nights if she was tired, old and new favorites, chosen haphazardly, each of us taking turns suggesting things, but somehow all our choices seemed resonant in their way. We watched David Byrne's brilliant musical *American Utopia*, which led us back to *Stop Making Sense*, the Talking Heads concert movie. We had seen it together in the theatre when it first came out, and I recalled how much it meant to Sue, the bass player, to see Tina Weymouth playing her instrument with such joyful exuberance.

We both loved *Enola Holmes*, the story of a young woman with two well-known brothers, Mycroft and Sherlock. I thought of Sue's vivid memory of our attorney father introducing my brother and me as his future law partners and having nothing to say about Sue, who was "shy." Enola might well have been overshadowed by her brothers' talents and accomplishments, overlooked in a society too-often indifferent to women's gifts, but somehow, through pluck and cunning and quiet determination, she finds and follows her own brave path.

We watched Frederick Wiseman's epic four-and-half hour

documentary *City Hall* over the better part of a week, scene after scene depicting the quiet, modest, never flashy good that public servants do—issuing licenses and performing marriages, filling potholes and picking up garbage, tending to the elderly, housing the vulnerable—and I couldn't help but recall Sue as an undergraduate student of public administration maintaining that yes, it just might be possible for public servants to make a difference in the lives of ordinary people.

And we both loved Armando Iannucci's *The Personal History of David Copperfield*, the story of a courageous and resilient young man surviving all manner of childhood hardship who, buoyed by the support and love of an endearingly eccentric but kind family of helpers, finds his voice and tells his story. I was reminded of Sue saying that her favorite literary themes were "overcoming tragedy" and "unconditional love." In the last scene of the film, Dev Patel as David Copperfield stands on stage and reads from his autobiographical novel. "This narrative is far more than fiction," David says. "It is written memory, wherein loss and love live forever side by side." Of course, I thought of Sue's story, her own written memory, its distinctive strands of loss and love.

Sue and I had completed the final edits of *The Crystal Gavel* in the months before her death. Earlier, we'd worked together on the book in person—at Northern Pine Lodge near Park Rapids, Minnesota, where our families used to vacation; at a cabin on Lake Ontario; and in Minneapolis during several of my visits. Sue would write and share pages with me, but we also played cribbage and usually she'd cook for us in her usual extravagant, improvisational, narrative style—a little of this, some more of that, only the best colorful ingredients, lots of tastes and exclamations.

In late 2020, in a series of long Zoom calls, we shared the manuscript on our screens and together went over every chapter, every line, every word. Sue had become a skillful and tireless reviser, always willing to go deeper. It seems to me that her Buddhist practice, her capacity, as Thich Nhat Hanh, says, "to look deeply into the nature of things," served her well. She revised the material about our parents many times, not content with easy or superficial portrayals of them. Yes, our father was a violent drunk, but Sue came to see him also as another suffering and damaged soul, struggling to find a language to express his own profound grief. In the early drafts of the book, Sue portrayed our mother as sick, depressed, and needy—which she was in her later years. But Sue came to believe she was much more than that and was determined to do justice to all of her—her creativity, her humor, her physical courage—and went back and wrote those beautiful descriptions of our mother gardening, cooking, arranging flowers, and later, in less stable and happy times, doing her best—her "utmost"—to keep us safe and pointed in the right direction.

It takes courage to write with such honesty not just about others but also yourself. Sue's long experience practicing the twelve steps of Alcoholics Anonymous—performing a searching and fearless moral inventory and admitting the exact nature of her wrongs—no doubt prepared her for this kind of self-scrutiny. Still, at first, while Sue wrote about her recovery from alcoholism with great vividness and particularity, her discussion of her actual drinking was mostly general and abstract. I may have cautiously suggested that readers, in order to fully understand her recovery, would want and need to know more about what she was recovering from. I knew this could be embarrassing, humiliating even, and painful. Sue nodded and went to work. By this time, she was a writer: She understood what the story required and was brave enough to do what needed to be done.

In those last Zoom sessions in late 2020, we addressed every note and did our best to remove every infelicity, obscurity, distraction, and false note. We picked every nit. We'd work for an hour or two, and, when I sensed Sue's energy flagging, I'd suggest we'd take it up again the next day. It was a talky, highly inefficient process, full of digressions, lots of laughter, and a few tears. Every story on the page—the happy and the harrowing ones from our childhood, her adventures in France, her courtroom and parenting anecdotes—seemed to evoke several more. We talked at length about some things for the first time, helped each other fill in some blanks in our personal and family histories.

I remember worrying a little at first about offering feedback to Sue, wondering how she might respond to her little brother giving her writing advice. Of course, she was a quick study. At one point, Sue became aware of something that those who loved her knew very well: She lived in a world of superlatives. Around Sue, food was the most delicious. When I cracked a joke, I was the wittiest fellow in America. If you gave Sue a gift, you were the most thoughtful, the most generous person ever. The magic of Sue was that in her presence, we all became our best selves. But in writing, it's a good idea to turn that down a little. And pretty soon, Sue got into the spirit of things, eventually finding and eliminating superlatives no one had even pointed out, sometimes more than one per page. It became one of our favorite running jokes. "I use the most superlatives of any writer ever!" I remember Sue saying. "But you are the best ever at fixing them," I told her.

For Sue, writing was a kind of return to her creative childhood self. When she was in grade school, one of her poems was published in *Highlights* magazine. Sue was something like eight years old at the time, and did not return to writing seriously until her fifties. She liked to say, with characteristic self-deprecating humor, that she had overcome one of the longest episodes of writer's block ever recorded.

Sue began writing stories of her life for herself, in the same spirit she played the guitar and took up quilting, simply for the intrinsic rewards of making something. She loved being a student, cultivating what Buddhists call the beginner's mind, practicing an art. She took classes at the Loft Literary Center in Minneapolis and the University of Iowa's Summer Writers' Festival; she took online courses and workshops; she worked for years with a writing coach.

She started writing short, short stories, fragmentary narratives, micro-memoir. After a while, her stories grew deeper and more layered; they started to coalesce, to form an arc. Sue began to see themes and patterns, ways that her personal journey informed her life's work. She saw how, for example, she struggled early on to find a voice, and then, in her courtroom, she strove to empower others to speak, to give them a genuine hearing.

Sue's intended audience was her three children. She knew that her time was limited and she wanted to leave them a full accounting of her life, in her own words. She wanted them to know who she was, what mattered to her. She had no fantasies of publication. Only later, little by little, did she come to believe that her story might be useful to others beyond her immediate family. Her experience in AA made her appreciate in a profound way the power of story: how both the telling and open-hearted receiving of another's story is transformative. She understood the unique power of stories to share experience, strength, and hope. It was part of her Buddhist practice to cultivate an awareness of and compassion for others, to extend herself to them. Sharing her story more widely, she came to believe, was a way to do that. Sue's legal career was cut short before she could fully bring about the transformation she so ardently believed the system needed. She hoped her story would inspire a new generation of lawyers and judges to make the courts more humane and compassionate. She believed her story might resonate with others who likewise struggled to find a voice, who sought healing from childhood trauma, struggled with alcoholism, faced parenting challenges, and ultimately, came to terms with their own mortality.

During one of our working sessions, I noticed among Sue's massive sheaf of notes and drafts, a kind of diagram—what she called a mind map. There's a heart in the middle of the page labeled "Meaning of Life" with a large question mark. Emanating from that heart are several arrows and word bubbles. "To find the meaning of life," one says. And: "To be kind." "To help others." "To help those who cannot help themselves." "To bring peace everywhere." "To embody love."

Leave it to Sue, I thought, to find five different ways to say pretty much the same thing—that love was the meaning of her life. By that point in her life, all her arrows were pointing outward. She embodied love as fully as any person I've ever met. I asked Sue if I could have the drawing, and she not only gave it to me, but signed it with a little heart. I had it framed and it now hangs above my desk where I am writing this.

Several months before her death, I promised Sue that I would see her book into print, and with her usual enthusiasm and legal savvy, she drafted and signed a document naming me her literary executor. Sue's book became part of the vast project of her life. It is a way that she continues, even now, to embody love.

The day after Sue died, I shared this with Sue's friends on her CaringBridge page:

> *There will always be a Sue-shaped hole in our hearts. We awoke this morning, her sons and I, for the first time to a world without Sue in it. And yet. We can hear her voice. We feel her presence. The boys know "what Mom would do." We are going to do our best, each in our way, to channel her loving and generous spirit. We can nurture all the goodness and strength she saw in us that we don't always see in ourselves.*

You can hear Sue's voice on every page of *The Crystal Gavel*. If you open your heart, you too will feel her presence, her compassion and courage, her generosity and joy, and come to feel, as I do, what a profound gift it is to know her.

ACKNOWLEDGMENTS

MY SISTER SUE WAS A genius of both generosity and gratitude. Someone who knew her well once commented, "Sue always receives more than we give her," and she was right. It grieves me that Sue did not have the chance to compose her own acknowledgments: what a joyful epic it would have been! I must be content with imperfectly sketching the contours of her gratitude as I knew it, trusting and hoping that all who loved and helped Sue will understand, whether or not they are named here explicitly, what their gifts to her meant and how deeply she appreciated them.

As a writer, Sue had many editors, teachers, and supportive readers, most notably her beloved writing coach Rosanne Bane, as well as Melanie Faith, Elizabeth Jarrett Andrew, Lon Otto, Diana Goetsch, and Carol Ann Fitzgerald.

Sue's Friday circle of friends, "The Peaceful Warriors," provided her immeasurable love and courage and camaraderie: Pavi Mehta, Pat Benincasa, Vara Bala Krishnan, Emily Barr, Liz Hernandez Pimental-Gopal, Vinya Sankaran Vasu, and Jane Jackson.

Common Ground Meditation Center in Minneapolis was a beloved spiritual home for Sue and she felt tremendous affection, admiration, and gratitude to the entire community, especially Mark Nunberg, Wynn Fricke, and Patricia Koelsch. As her memoir makes clear, Sue believed that the twelve-step fellowship of Alcoholics Anonymous saved her life: She felt love and gratitude for every single person she met while trudging "the Road of Happy Destiny."

Organizing a symposium supported by the Fetzer Foundation devoted to bringing compassion into the law—what Sue liked to refer to informally as "the love conference"—was a profoundly meaningful experience and she was grateful beyond words to Ron Ousky for inviting her to co-design and co-organize it, to Tara Brach and the late Cheri Maples for giving inspirational keynotes, to Barbara McAfee for facilitating so beautifully, and to all the leaders and innovators from across the world who came to contribute.

Sue lived a full and energetic and joyful life for more than a decade with a Stage 4 diagnosis, and she appreciated the scores of medical professionals who cared for her with incredible expertise and compassion—doctors, all manner of specialists, nurses, technicians, aides, and receptionists—she knew their names, shared their stories, and was grateful for their countless kindnesses. Dr. Robert Spetzler at Barrow Neurological Institute removed a brain tumor that other surgeons had deemed inoperable and added years to her life: Sue considered what he did nothing short of miraculous. Sue credited Dr. Joseph Leach of Minnesota Oncology with extending her life—and enriching it with his friendship. Sue's health and healing were likewise nurtured profoundly by her retreat at and ongoing connection to Commonweal in California: its president and cofounder Michael Lerner was a source of wisdom and solace, and Dr. Rachel Naomi Remen, Medical Director of Commonweal Cancer Help Program, was a hero of Sue's, her *Kitchen Table Wisdom* an important influence on Sue's thinking about the courts and an inspiration for *The Crystal Gavel*. Sue promoted her own physical, emotional, artistic, and spiritual well-being and growth through innumerable healings, workshops, treatments, lessons, and therapeutic sessions, and felt tremendous respect and gratitude for every single one of her teachers, healers, and caregivers, among them Nancy Cox, Janet

Hovde, Emily Jarrett Hughes, Bob Schmitt, and the therapists at Unwind Within.

Throughout the course of her life, from her earliest days at Brady High School and the Snyder lunch counter in West St. Paul, through college and law school and her legal career, during her journey to sobriety, serenity and peacefulness, right until her last visit to her oncologist's office, Sue made friends. She was especially grateful for all those who comprised her vast and loving CaringBridge community: They read and "hearted" her posts and day after day, week after week, month after month, made her feel, to quote a favorite Raymond Carver poem, "beloved on the earth." These friends enriched Sue's life immeasurably: They laughed and cried with her, shared their stories, brought her food, and in a thousand ways brought joy and connection and meaning to her life. Here is a highly selective roll call of their names: Carol Aker, Delma Bartelme, Gloria Bogen, Karmit Bulman, Kevin Burke, the late Linda Byrne, David Carr, Ann Chapman, Mary Christenson, Colleen Corrigan, Victoria Crawford, Marybeth Dorn, Barb Dunn, Lilian Ejebe, Muggsy Ferber, Marjorie Fitzsimmons, Terry Gibson, Tia Karelson, Jeanne Karnowski, Talia Katz, Eve Keepings de Jesus, Jim Laurence, Ann Leppanen, Marsha and Dan Loewenson, Leslie Masterson, Sue Mauer, Marcy Miller, Kate Milligan, Tim Mulrooney, David Piper, Jody Remsing, Denice Robertson, John and Kelly Schupp, Azure Snyder, Dan Simon, Danette Tenney, Patty Theobald, Colleen and Leif Ueland, the late Paul Von Drasek, Lisa Von Drasek, Ellen Weinberg, Jan Werness, Jack Williams, and Mary Wilmes.

Only after Sue's death did I learn that Sue had sent an inquiry to Wise Ink about the possibility of publishing *The Crystal Gavel*. When I learned this, I thought, yes, of course: "Authors with purpose, books with soul." The Wise Ink team, in particular Victoria Petelin, has been unfailingly professional, skillful, and kind. Sue would have loved working with them—and how they would have loved working with her!—and Sue would have loved how beautifully they helped to realize her creative vision.

Sue would have concluded with deep, heartfelt, and ultimately immeasurable and inexpressible gratitude and love for her family. She would have thanked me extravagantly, I know that, as well as my wife, Mary Cochrane, Sue's sister-in-law, a friend for the long haul, through decades of laughter and tears, and finally, as an editor extraordinaire, the last loving set of eyes on her book. Sue would have found a way to express how deeply she loved and appreciated our cousin Kris Frykman, whom she called her soul sister—artist and healer and loving companion every single step of the way.

Last, and always, in all ways, Sue would have expressed her never-ending and unconditional love for her own immediate family, her husband Clair and sons Lee, Tom, and Sunny. This book is her gift to them.

Mick Cochrane
Buffalo, NY
April 2023

SUE COCHRANE was born and raised in West St. Paul, Minnesota, and earned a BA in French and political science from Hamline University and a JD from William Mitchell College of Law. She served for eighteen years on the family court bench in Minneapolis, where she pioneered a holistic and humane approach to conflict resolution. Previously, she had a private practice and was an attorney for Legal Aid at the Native American Center in St. Paul. When diagnosed with Stage 4 breast cancer, Sue retired from the bench, but lived joyfully for ten more years, writing and speaking, devoting herself to family and friends, making art and practicing Buddhism, and co-chairing an international symposium supported by the Fetzer Institute that focused on bringing love, compassion, and forgiveness into the law. She died on February 13, 2021.

MICK COCHRANE, Sue's younger brother, earned degrees from the University of St. Thomas and the University of Minnesota and is professor of English at Canisius University in Buffalo, NY. He is the author of four novels and has published stories, essays, and poems in numerous journals and anthologies. You can visit him at **mickcochrane.com**.